CRYPTOGRAPHY

AUTHOR

DR. PRATIK VANJARA

CRYPTOGRAPHY

AUTHOR

DR. PRATIK VANJARA

No part of this book may be reproduced or utilized in any form or by any means,

Electronic or mechanical including photocopying recording

Or by any information storage and retrieval system

Without permission in writing.

Inquiries should be addressed to

Dr.Pratik A Vanjara

c103,padmavati residency,

gautam nagar main road,

opp sterling hospital,gandhigram,Rajkot

Email: 369pratik@gmail.com

Copy: 100

Price: 250

First Edition (December-2015)

ISBN NO : *978-93-84644-32-1*

DEDICATED

TO

My Mother

A strong and gentle soul who taught me to trust in GOD,

Believe in hard work and that so much could be done with

little

My Father

For being my first teacher

My wife

For earning honest living for us and for supporting

and encouraging me to believe in myself

Preface

This book is intended as a reference for professional cryptographers, presenting the techniques and algorithms of greatest interest to the current practitioner, along with the supporting motivation and background material. It also provides a comprehensive source from which to learn cryptography, serving both students and instructors. In addition, the rigorous treatment, breadth, and extensive bibliographic material should make it an important reference for research professionals.

Our goal was to assimilate the existing cryptographic knowledge of industrial interest into one consistent, self-contained volume accessible to engineers in practice, to computer scientists and mathematicians in academia, and to motivated non-specialists with a strong desire to learn cryptography. Such a task is beyond the scope of each of the following: research papers, which by nature focus on narrow topics using very specialized (and often non-standard) terminology; survey papers, which typically address, at most, a small number of major topics at a high level; and (regrettably also) most books, due to the fact that many book authors lack either practical experience or familiarity with the research literature or both. Our intent was to provide a detailed presentation of those areas of cryptography which we have found to be of greatest practical utility in our own industrial experience, while maintaining a sufficiently formal approach to be suitable both as a trustworthy reference for those whose primary interest is further research, and to provide a solid foundation for students and others first learning the subject.

Throughout each chapter, we emphasize the relationship between various aspects of cryptography. Background sections commence most chapters, providing a framework and perspective for the techniques which follow. Computer source code (e.g. C code) for algorithms has been intentionally omitted, in favor of algorithms specified in sufficient detail to allow direct implementation without consulting secondary references. We believe this style of presentation allows a better understanding of how algorithms actually work, while at the same time avoiding low-level implementation-specific constructs (which some readers will invariably be unfamiliar with) of various currently-popular programming languages.

The presentation also strongly delineates what has been established as fact (by mathematical arguments) from what is simply current conjecture. To avoid obscuring the very applied nature of the subject, rigorous proofs of correctness are in most cases omitted; however, references given in the Notes section at the end of each chapter indicate the original or recommended sources for these results. The trailing Notes sections also provide information (quite detailed in places) on various additional techniques not addressed in the main text, and provide a survey of research activities and theoretical results; references again indicate where readers may pursue particular aspects in greater depth. Needless to say, many results, and indeed some entire research areas, have been given far less attention than they warrant, or have been omitted entirely due to lack of space; we apologize in advance for such major omissions, and hope that the most significant of these are brought to our attention.

Each chapter was written to provide a self-contained treatment of one major topic. Collectively, however, the chapters have been designed and carefully integrated to be entirely complementary with respect to definitions, terminology, and notation. Furthermore, there is essentially no duplication of material across chapters; instead, appropriate cross-chapter references are provided where relevant.

While it is not intended that this book be read linearly from front to back, the material has been arranged so that doing so has some merit. Two primary goals motivated by the "handbook" nature of this project were to allow easy access to stand-alone results, and to allow results and algorithms to be easily referenced (e.g., for discussion or subsequent cross-reference). To facilitate the ease of accessing and referencing results, items have been categorized and numbered to a large extent, with the following classes of items jointly numbered consecutively in each chapter: *Definitions, Examples, Facts, Notes, Remarks, Algorithms, Protocols,* and *Mechanisms.* In more traditional treatments, *Facts* are usually identified as propositions, lemmas, or theorems. We use numbered *Notes* for additional technical points, while numbered *Remarks* identify non-technical (often non-rigorous) comments, observations, and opinions. *Algorithms, Protocols* and *Mechanisms* refer to techniques involving a series of steps. *Examples, Notes,* and *Remarks* generally begin with parenthetical summary titles to allow faster access, by indicating the nature of the content so that the entire item itself need not be read in order to determine this. The use of a large number of small subsections is also intended to enhance the handbook nature and accessibility to results.

Regarding the partitioning of subject areas into chapters, we have used what we call a *functional organization* (based on functions of interest to end-users). For example, all items related to entity authentication are addressed in one chapter. An alternative would have been what may be called an *academic organization*, under which perhaps, all protocols based on zero-knowledge concepts (including both a subset of entity authentication protocols and signature schemes) might be covered in one chapter. We believe that a functional organization is more convenient to the practitioner, who is more likely to be interested in options available for an entity authentication protocol (Chapter 10) or a signature scheme (Chapter 11), than to be seeking a zero-knowledge protocol with unspecified end-purpose.

In most cases (with some historical exceptions), where algorithms are known to be insecure, we have chosen to leave out specification of their details, because most such techniques are of little practical interest. Essentially all of the algorithms included have been verified for correctness by independent implementation, confirming the test vectors specified.

Any errors that remain are, of course, entirely our own. We would be grateful if readers who spot errors, missing references or credits, or incorrectly attributed results would contact us with details. It is our hope that this volume facilitates further advancement of the field, and that we have helped play a small part in this.

Contents

List of Figures

List of Tables

	Bit Wise comparisons
5.9	Windows 8 Encryption and Decryption time of Character wise files Bit Wise comparisons
5.10	Windows 8 Encryption and Decryption time of Line wise files Bit Wise comparisons
5.11	Windows 8 Encryption and Decryption time of Paragraph files Bit Wise comparisons

Chapter -1

Introduction
1.1 Research Objective

The main objective of this research is to study various cryptography algorithms, comparison and its analysis statistically, a model would be suggested for Cryptography for data Encryption and Decryption.

I would like to suggest a model for cryptography which provides security for any kind of data like Text, Image, Audio, Video etc. An algorithm based on model will be compared with RSA algorithm, ELGAMAL algorithm and DSA algorithm.

This model will work with character data, image data and audio data, it will be compared with various operating systems for performance measurement and then statistical analysis will show the result of comparison.

The aim of this research work is to suggest a model for all kind of encryption and decryption for more security in less amount of time.

1.2 Statement of the title

ANALYSIS AND DESIGN OF CRYPTOGRAPHIC ALGORITHMS

1.3 The research Area and problem definition

Cryptography algorithm working with two resources encryption and decryption, with this reference we can check different aspect like Time (Minute, Second) and cipher key language in different machines.

In cryptography, the security of most systems necessarily relies upon computational problems that are conjectured to be intractable, i.e., infeasible to solve with any realistic amount of computational resources. Over the past three decades, the most useful candidate hard problems have come from an area of mathematics called number theory. For instance, a commonly made conjecture is that it is infeasible to compute the prime factors of huge random integers. However, the relatively high computational cost, and largely sequential nature, of operating on such enormous numbers inherently limits the efficiency and applicability of numbertheoretic cryptography. Even more worrisome is that quantum algorithms, which work in a model of computation that exploits quantum mechanics to dramatically speed up certain kinds of computations, can efficiently solve all the number-theoretic problems commonly used in cryptography! Therefore, the future development of a practical, large-scale quantum computer would be devastating to the security of today's cryptographic systems. Alternative foundations are therefore sorely needed.

There are many security algorithm available, algorithm require more power to compute the result and the ones which require less computational power are easy to crack. To overcome the drawbacks of existing system, an algorithm is developed keeping in mind the high security and less computational power.

1.4 Relevance of research

I have study many algorithm related cryptography and design new algorithm that can be used for Data Encryption and decryption for all type of security applications.

In today's world security of information is a fundamental necessity not only for military and diplomatic messages but also for private communication. Today's era of communication has increased the importance of financial data exchange, image processing, biometrics and e-commerce transactions which in turn has made data security an important issue. Cryptography is defended as the science concerned with communications in security form. The goal of cryptography is the construction of schemes, which can maintain desired security, even after malicious attempts have been made. Cryptography consists of cryptography and cryptanalysis. The former involves the study and application of various techniques through which information may be rendered unintelligible to all breaking cryptosystems and recovering the secret information.

Recently, there has been a shift of focus in cryptography. Today's cryptography not only provides confidentiality, authentication, data integrity and non repudiation, but has also the added task of providing security in menacing environments. Cryptology is a strange field of science. As opposed works against a powerful, malicious adversary, often referred to as the eaves-dropper. The adversary attacking the system will try to manipulate the environment into conducive states and try to break the system by adopting strategies which the designer may have not envisioned. For the attacker it suffices to show a single successful weakness of the cryptosystem. A secured cryptosystem has to withstand all such types of attacks. This tussle between the cryptographer and the cryptanalysis has continued for ages.

1.5 Details of Remaining Chapters

The researcher has distributed the entire work into five different chapters. The chapter summary for the remaining chapter i.e. from chapter-2 to chapter-5 is as follow

Chapter 1 Introduction

This chapter contains introduction of cryptography, algorithm research problem, objective etc.

Chapter 2 Introduction of Cryptography

This chapter contains introduction of cryptography, it contains definition of cryptography algorithm, its needs and other basic detail.

Chapter 3 Analysis of Algorithms

This chapter describes the basic Private Key Algorithms. It also focuses on the different techniques for extracting, storing, comparing different features of Cryptography algorithms (DSA, RSA and ELGAMAL). The researcher has also discussed the different Algorithms processing tools to manage varies tasks of Algorithms. Comparison of various algorithms was carried out on the bit length criteria for 512 bits, 1024 bits and 2048 bits. Each of this bit length data were analyzed Character wise, Line wise & Paragraph wise. Variance analysis was performed for this data. Correlation between algorithms was established and correlation coefficients are calculated. After obtaining results a variance table and a correlation coefficient table are constructed.

Chapter – 3 Analyses of Algorithms

By keenly studying the different characteristics and tools described in chapter-2, the researcher has proposed a model for Private Key Algorithm and also described the functionalities of each components of the model. Initially the advantages and limitations of all the algorithms are mentioned. Design specifications of the new algorithm are mentioned. The entire algorithm development process is described in detail and DFD and ER diagrams are constructed to support the development of new algorithm. The detailed steps of both encryption and decryption algorithm are mentioned. In order to understand the impact of newly developed algorithm on RSA, DSA and ELGAMAL, multiple correlation coefficients are calculated in various operating systems and for different bit length data.

Chapter – 4 Design, Model & of Public Key Algorithm

The chapter is concerned with an experimental prototype of the model already proposed in the chapter-3. The researcher has developed the different components of the model. The data was taken by the algorithm for its experiential validation. Strength and complexity of the algorithm is tested by testing it for avalanche effect and performing security analysis. The final result of the PK algorithm for the input data is mentioned and special features of this algorithm are listed out.

Chapter – 5 Summary and Future work

All the chapters which are previously mentioned are well summarized in Chapter 5. The details of all the chapters individually are mentioned. The entire development process of the new PK algorithm which is developed with the help of DSA, RSA and ELGAMAL algorithm is summarized in this chapter. As a conclusion, the need of this algorithm, its efficiency compared to the already existing algorithm and details about the current trends and future trends in the field of data security is mentioned. the scope of expansion of the already developed PK algorithm. The future of technology is approaching with a rapid rate and therefore the adaptability of current technologies with future ones is absolutely vital. This chapter specifies what specific work can be done on this algorithm for future work.

Chapter -2

Introduction of Cryptography

Many people think of cryptography as spies trading secret messages written with strange symbols that only the author and recipient of the message can understand. Therefore, they tend to be unaware of the impact cryptography has had on the world and on their daily lives. However, it has become available for anyone to make use of, not just for government communications and professionals, especially in terms of E-Commerce and online payments. This essay discusses what cryptography is, its primitives, its encryption algorithms and why we need it. Furthermore, it analyzes the cryptography historically and the needs for algorithms development that led currently to Public Key Infrastructures and authorities demands for the sake of having more authentic and secure transactions.[1]

Cryptography is a successful academic discipline relating a combine of arithmetic, figures and computer Science" . Cryptography is a skill of transforming information so it is secure while being stored or spread over the Computer network. [1]

In cryptography algorithms are two basic types of symmetric algorithms: block ciphers and stream ciphers. This algorithm of Block ciphers operate on blocks of plaintext and ciphertext—usually of 64 bits but sometimes longer. Stream ciphers work on streams of plaintext and ciphertext one bit or byte (sometimes even one 32-bit word) moment in time. With a block cipher, the same plaintext block will always encrypt to the same ciphertext block by means of the equivalent key. The stream ciphers the similar plaintext bit or byte will encrypt to a different bit or byte every time it is encrypted. [2]

A cryptographic mode usually combines the basic cipher and some category of response, and some plain operations. This operation is simple because the security is a function of the underlying cipher and not the method. Yet more strongly the cipher mode should not compromise the security of the underlying algorithm.[3]

There are other security considerations: Patterns in the plaintext should be hidden, key to the cipher should be randomized and manipulation of the plaintext by introduce errors in the ciphertext should be complicated; encryption have more than one message with the same key should be possible. Effectiveness is a dissimilar concern. The mode should not be significantly less efficient than the original cipher. A few condition it is significant that the ciphertext be the same size as the plaintext. A third consideration is fault-tolerance. A few applications need to parallelize encryption or decryption the others side need to be able to preprocess as a huge amount of data possible. In still others it is important that the decrypting process be able to recover from bit errors in the ciphertext stream, or dropped or added bits.[2]

2.1 Early vs. Modern Cryptography

Cryptography technology is very much more difficult than its predecessor. In today the original use of cryptography in its standard roots where it was implemented to hide both diplomatic and military secrets from the opponent, even though it still has far-reaching military implications has expanded its area and has been designed to provide a cost-effective means of securing and thus protecting large amounts of electronic data that is stored and communicated across network universal. Cryptography offers the means for protecting this data all the while preserving the security of critical personal financial, medical, and ecommerce data that might end up in the hands of those who shouldn't have access to it.[4]

There have been many advances in the area of modern cryptography that have emerged beginning in the 1970s as the development of strong encryption-based protocols and newly developed cryptographic applications began to appear on the scene., the National Bureau of Standards (NBS) adopted a data encryption standard called the Data Encryption Standard (DES), which was a milestone in launching cryptography research and development into the modern age of computing skill. cryptography found its way into the commercial field when, on December, 1980, the same algorithm, DES, was adopted by the American National Standards Institute (ANSI). Following this milestone was yet another when a new concept was proposed to develop Public Key Cryptography (PKC), which is still undergoing research development today (Levy, 2001).[4]

Cryptography is considered not only a part of the branch of mathematics, but also a branch of computer science. There are two forms of cryptosystems: symmetric and asymmetric. Symmetric cryptosystems involve the use of a single key known as the secret key to encrypt and decrypt data or messages. Asymmetric cryptosystems, on the other hand, use one key (the public key) to encrypt messages or data, and a second key (the secret key) to decipher or decrypt those messages or data. For this reason, asymmetric cryptosystems are also known as public key cryptosystems. The problem that symmetric cryptosystems have always faced is the lack of a secure means for the sharing of the secret key by the individuals who wish to secure their data or communications. Public key cryptosystems solve this problem through the use of cryptographic algorithms used to create the public key and the secret key, such as DES, which has already been mentioned, and a much stronger algorithm, RSA. The RSA algorithm is the most popular form of public key cryptosystem, which was developed by Ron Rivest, Adi Shamir, and Leonard Adleman at the Massachusetts Institute of Technology in 1977 (Robinson, 2008). The RSA algorithm involves the process of generating the public key by multiplying two very large (100 digits or more) randomly chosen prime numbers, and then, by randomly choosing another very large number, called the encryption key. The public key would then consist of both the encryption key and the product of those two primes. Ron Rivest then developed a simple formula by which someone who wanted to scramble a message could use that public key to do so. The plaintext would then be converted to ciphertext, which was transformed by an equation that included that large product. Lastly, using an algorithm developed through the work of the great mathematician, Euclid, Ron Rivest provided for a decryption key—one that could only be calculated by the use of the original two prime numbers. Using this encryption key would unravel the ciphertext and transform it back into its original plaintext. What makes the RSA algorithm strong is the mathematics that is involved. Ascertaining the original randomly chosen prime numbers and the large randomly chosen number (encryption key) that was used to form the product that encrypted the data in the first place is nearly impossible (Levy, 2001).[4]

A very popular public key cryptosystem is known as Pretty Good Privacy (PGP), developed by Phil Zimmerman beginning in early 1991 (Levy, 2001). The strength of the keys that are created to encrypt and decrypt data or communications is a function of the length of those keys. Typically the longer the key, the stronger that key is. For example, a 56-bit key (consisting of 56 bits of data) would not be as strong as a 128-bit key. And, consequently, a 128-bit key would not be as strong as a 256- or 1024-bit key. [4]

2.2 Ciphertext

In cryptography, ciphertext (or cyphertext) is the result of encryption performed on plaintext using an algorithm, called a cipher. Ciphertext is also known as encrypted or encoded information because it contains a form of the original plaintext that is unreadable by a human or computer without the proper cipher to decrypt it. Decryption, the inverse of encryption, is the process of turning ciphertext into readable plaintext. Ciphertext is not to be confused with codetext because the latter is a result of a code, not a cipher.[5]

2.3 Need of Cryptography/Encryption:

- Increased volume of communication over insecure channels.
- Increased requirements for remote access to information.
- Regulatory requirements for data protection.
- Needs for an electronic equivalent to hand-written signature

2.4 Cryptography Properties
Access Control: Deny access for the "unauthorized" people.[1]

Security Definitions
The terms "secure" and "break the system" quite loosely. What do we really mean? It is clear that a minimal requirement of security would be that: any adversary who can see the ciphertext and knows which encryption and decryption algorithms are being used, can not recover the entire cleartext. But, many more properties may be desirable. To name a few:
1. It should be hard to recover the messages from the ciphertext when the messages are drawn from random probability distributions defined on the set of all strings (i.e random message spaces). A few examples of message spaces are: the English language, the set $\{0, 1\}$.
2. It should be hard to compute incomplete information about messages from the ciphertext.
3. It should be hard to detect simple but useful facts about traffic of messages, such as when the same message is sent twice.
4. The above properties should hold with high probability.
In short, it would be desirable for the encryption scheme to be the mathematical analogy of opaque envelopes containing a piece of paper on which the message is written. The envelopes should be such that all legal senders can fill it, but only the legal recipient can open it.[6]
2.5 Literature review for the study
The main objective of the present study was: *"To Analysis and develop cryptography algorithms"*. The researcher had studied a lot of related literature to identify the different works done in the related area. The study had given a more clear vision in the task. In this present chapter, the brief information about the related research works for the present study is given

A glance over related literature
Initial computers were design just to do simple calculations; scientists have been trying to endow the computer with more and more intelligence.

That is to make the digital machine, do things, which require human-like intelligence. Thus the term Artificial Intelligence (AI) was coined in early 1950s. Gradually scientists came to know the immense power of the device and its limitations. More and more systems have been developed as a consequence of incremental advances in computer science. Slowly these electronics devices have been spreading their roots in the soils of this society. Now computer systems are available for applications of civil amenities to medical diagnosis; home entertainment to space programs; simple calculations to complex mathematical modeling etc.[7]

In today's fast placed world where every human being has to combat a race against time – a direct interface between the security and computer user will gleefully accept the same text typed on the computer screen with minimum lapse of time. The phenomenon is known as cryptography.

Now that we have analyzed some of the research that has been conducted and reported in scholarly literature, let's switch our focus and review some of the non-scholarly literature that has been published on this topic as well.

Chapter -3

Analysis of Algorithms

3.1 PRIVATE KEY ALGORITHMS
3.1.1 DES Algorithm

Data encryption standard (DES) is a modern method of cryptography the national institute of standard and technology (NIST) is agency, which approved that DES is an old encryption algorithm created in the mid 1970s.[8]

DES is block cipher, which consists with a 64 bit block size, a 56 bit keys and also consists of a 16 round series of substitution and permutation each round of DES are shifted that means data and key bits are shifted with each they. In DES algorithms, permutated, XORED, and sent through 8 s-boxes, a set of lookup tables are very important Description is the same process like DES, but it is performed in reverse. Many controversies are crossed for DES particular for design elements short key, length of the symmetric key, block cipher design and nourishing suspicions about a backdoor.[8]

DES is considered to be insecure for many application because of the 56 bit key size being two small for it. distributed.net and EFFC (The Electronic frontier foundation collaborated) to publicly break a DES key in 22 hours and 15 minutes in January 1999. some analytical results declared or approved that some theoretical weaknesses in the cipher, and it is also infeasible to mount in practice, In the form of triple DES, the algorithms is practically secure although there are theoretical attacks on the algorithms. now a days, AES (advanced encryption standard) has been superseded the block cipher.[9]

Key Generation

FACTORS	DES
Key Length	56 bits
Block Size	64 bits
Cipher Text	Symmetric block cipher
Developed	1977
Security	Proven inadequate
Cryptanalysis Resistance	Vulnerable to differential and linear cryptanalysis; weak substitution tables
Possible Keys	2^{56}
Possible ASCII Printable Character Key	95^7

3.1.2 Algorithms

Encryption:

STEP 1
- DES takes an input of 64-bit long plaintext and 56-bit key (8 bits of parity) and generates output of 64 bit block.
- The plaintext block is subject to an shift the bits around.
- The 8 parity bits are removed from the key by subjecting the key to its Key Permutation.
- The plaintext and key are processed in 16 rounds consisting of

STEP 2
- The key is written in different columns and provide columns number. Which means provide alphabetic order

STEP-3
- Write the plan text row by row

STEP-4
- Read that text column by column.

STEP-5
- After complete this steps the result is generated cipher text.

Decryption:
STEP 1
- In decryption means the text is changed in cipher text to plan text.

STEP 2
- The key is written in different column and provide column number.

STEP 3
- Write the cipher text in a group of characters in row format with proper number format.

STEP 4
- After complete all these steps, get the plaintext which return in a single row

3.1.3 Block Ciphers Features

Block size: in general larger block sizes mean greater security.
• Key size: larger key size means greater security (larger key space).
• Number of rounds: multiple rounds offer increasing security.
• Encryption modes: define how messages larger than the block size are encrypted, very important for the security of the encrypted message.[10]

3.2 PUBLIC KEY ALGORITHMS

3.2.1 RSA Algorithm

The RSA algorithm was invented by Ronald L. Rivest, Adi Shamir, and Leonard Adleman in 1977and released into the public domain on September 6, 2000.

Public-key systems–or asymmetric cryptography–use two different keys with a mathematical relationship to each other. Their protection relies on the premise that knowing one key will not help you figure out the other. The RSA algorithm uses the fact that it's easy to multiply two large prime numbers together and get a product. But you can't take that product and reasonably guess the two original numbers, or guess one of the original primes if only the other is known. The public key and private keys are carefully generated using the RSA algorithm; they can be used to encrypt information or sign it.[11]

RSA Key generation Algorithm
1) Pick two large prime numbers p and q
2) Calculate n = p × q;
3) Calculate $\varphi(n) = (p - 1)(q - 1)$;
4) Assume e such that $1 < e < \varphi(n)$ and e and n are co prime.
5) Compute a value for d such that $(d*e) \% \varphi(n) = 1$

Encryption

Alice transmits her public key (n,e) to Bob and keeps the private key secret. Bob then wishes to send message *M* to Alice.

He first turns *M* into an integer *m*, such that $0 \leq m \leq n$ by using an agreed-upon reversible protocol known as a padding scheme. he then computes the ciphertext *c* corresponding to

$c = m^e \pmod{n}$

This can be done quickly using the method of exponentiation by squaring. Bob then transmits *c* to Alice

Decryption

Alice can recover *m* from *c* by using her private key exponent *d* via computing.

$m = c^e \pmod{n}$

Given *m,* she can recover the original message *M* by reversing the padding scheme.

3.2.2 Elgamal Algorithm

Another algorithm based on exponentiation and modular arithmetic. ElGamal may be used for encryption and digital signatures in a manner similar to the RSA algorithm. Longer keys are generally considered to be more secure.[12]

In cryptography, the Elgamal encryption system is an asymmetric key encryption algorithm for public-key cryptography which is based on the Diffie–Hellman key exchange. It was described by Taher Elgamal in 1984. ElGamal encryption is used in the free GNU Privacy Guard software, recent versions of PGP, and other cryptosystems. The Digital Signature Algorithm is a variant of the ElGamal signature scheme, which should not be confused with ElGamal encryption.[13]

Each user has a private key x

•Each user has three public keys: prime modulus p, generator g and public Y = gxmod p

•Security is based on the difficulty of DLP

•Secure key size > 1024 bits

•Elgamal is quite slow, it is used mainly for key authentication protocols

•Now widely used, but Elliptic Curve variant is increasingly popular

3.2.3 DSA Algorithm

DSA is a United States Federal Government standard for digital signatures. It was proposed by the National Institute of Standards and Technology (NIST) in August 1991 for use in their Digital Signature Standard (DSS), specified in FIPS 186 in 1993. [14]

The first part of the DSA algorithm is the public key and private key generation, which can be described as:

- Choose a prime number q, which is called the prime divisor.
- Choose another primer number p, such that p-1 mod q = 0. p is called the prime modulus.
- Choose an integer g, such that 1 < g < p, g**q mod p = 1 and g = h**((p–1)/q) mod p. q is also called g's multiplicative order modulo p.
- Choose an integer, such that 0 < x < q.
- Compute y as g**x mod p.
- Package the public key as {p,q,g,y}.
- Package the private key as {p,q,g,x}

The second part of the DSA algorithm is the signature generation and signature verification, which can be described as:

To generate a message signature, the sender can follow these steps:

- Generate the message digest h, using a hash algorithm like SHA1.
- Generate a random number k, such that $0 < k < q$.
- Compute r as (g**k mod p) mod q. If r = 0, select a different k.
- Compute i, such that k*i mod q = 1. i is called the modular multiplicative inverse of k modulo q.
- Compute s = i*(h+r*x) mod q. If s = 0, select a different k.
- Package the digital signature as {r,s}.

To verify a message signature, the receiver of the message and the digital signature can follow these steps:

- Generate the message digest h, using the same hash algorithm.
- Compute w, such that s*w mod q = 1. w is called the modular multiplicative inverse of s modulo q.
- Compute u1 = h*w mod q.
- Compute u2 = r*w mod q.
- Compute v = (((g**u1)*(y**u2)) mod p) mod q.
- If v == r, the digital signature is valid. [14]

3.2.4 COMPARISION OF THIS ALGORITHM

Operating System: Operating systems are an essential part of any computer system. We have used various operating system such as Windows XP, Windows 7, Windows 8 in order to compress various Algorithm. So that we can find out the effect of output at system level. It will be also useful for design and implementation of Algorithm with necessary changes. We can note down time, latency between various OS.

Software: Java is a widely used programming language with a rich API and built-in language support for thread creation and management. Java programs run on any operating system supporting a Java virtual machine (or JVM). We illustrate various operating system and networking concepts with several Java programs tested using the Java 1.4 JVM NetBeans IDE 8.0.2

We have chosen these programming environments because it is our opinion that they best represent the most popular models of operating system: Windows, along with the widely used Java environment. Most programming examples are written in JAVA.

Hardware: During the course of this research, various tests have been carried out keeping the following hardware configuration in effect. Following are the minimum requirement specification for the algorithm:

<u>Windows 8</u>

1 GHz 32-bit (x86)

1 GB of system memory

16 GB available hard drive space (32-bit), 20 GB available hard drive space (64-bit)
DirectX 9 graphics device with WDDM 1.0 or higher driver
DVD-ROM drive
Audio Output

<u>Windows 7</u>
1 GHz 32-bit (x86)
1 GB of system memory
16 GB available hard drive space (32-bit), 20 GB available hard drive space (64-bit)
DirectX 9 graphics device with WDDM 1.0 or higher driver
DVD-ROM drive
Audio Output

<u>Windows XP Home & XP Professional</u>
Pentium 233 MHz processor (300 MHz is recommended)
at least 64 MB of RAM (128 MB is recommended)
at least 1.5 GB of available hard-disk space
CD-ROM drive

Input data size- Different algorithm requires different memory space to perform the operation. The memory space required by any algorithm is determined on the basis of input data size, number of rounds etc. The algorithm is considered best which uses less memory and performs best task.

Time- The time required by algorithm to complete the operation depends on processor speed, algorithm complexity. Lesser the time an algorithm takes to complete its operation better it is.

Bit Length- Different algorithms (RSA, DSA, ELGAMAL) require different bit length to perform the operation. In this analysis we compare different bit length like 512, 1024 and 2048.

Mean – Mean is a set of numeric values, as calculated by adding all values and divided by the number of terms in a set. Mean is calculated for further processing.

$$\bar{x} = \frac{\sum_{i=1}^{n} x_i}{n}$$

Variance – Variance is a measurement of spread between numbers in the data set, variance is always positive. A small value of variance indicates that the data point tends to be very close to the mean while high variance indicates that the data points are very spread out around the mean and from each other.

$$\sigma^2 = \frac{\sum_{i=1}^{n} (x_i - \bar{x})^2}{n}$$

Correlation – correlation is a relation between two variables, with cause and effect. If the changes in the values of two variables are simultaneous and when one changes due to the changes in other, the variables are said to be correlated. [15]

$$r = \frac{\sum xy - \sum x . \sum y}{(\sqrt{n \sum x^2 - (\sum x)^2} . (\sqrt{n \sum y^2 - (\sum y)^2})}$$

3.3 Variance analysis for various algorithms
Windows XP

1) **Character wise**
   - 512 Bit Length

SAMPLE	RSA	DSA	ELGAMAL
1	2	2	3
2	4	2	2
3	2	2	1
4	1	2	1
5	1	2	2
MEAN	**2**	**2**	**1.8**
VARIANCE	**1.5**	**0**	**0.7**

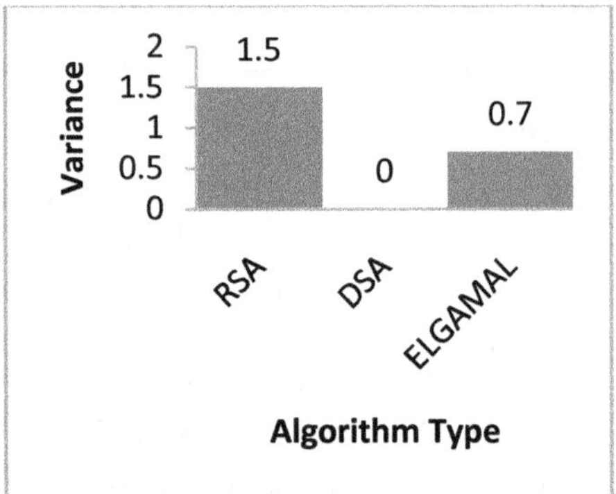

Figure 3.1

In this analysis minimum variance is zero for the DSA algorithm; compared to other algorithms DSA is consistent

   - 1024 bit length

Windows XP BITLENGTH 1024			
SAMPLE	RSA	DSA	ELGAMAL
1	3	2	2
2	5	2	4
3	3	2	3
4	2	3	2
5	4	2	2
MEAN	**3.4**	**2.2**	**2.6**
VARIANCE	**1.3**	**0.2**	**0.8**

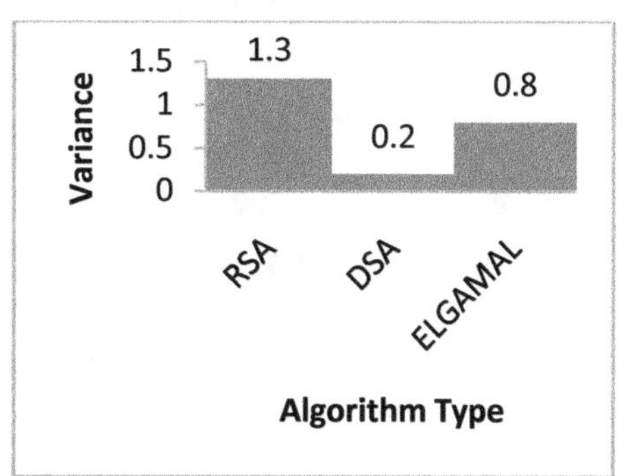

Figure 3.2

In this analysis minimum variance is 0.2 for the DSA algorithm; compared to other algorithms DSA is consistent.

- 2048 bit length

SAMPLE	RSA	DSA	ELGAMAL
1	57	2	22
2	11	1	19
3	75	2	35
4	28	1	52
5	17	2	14
MEAN	**37.6**	**1.6**	**28.4**
VARIANCE	**749.8**	**0.3**	**234.3**

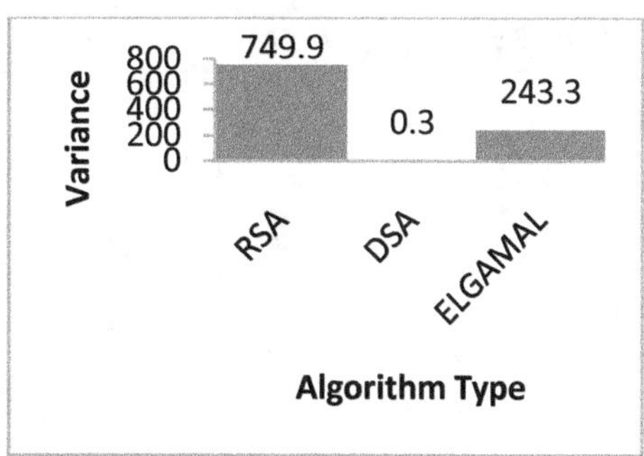

Figure 3.3

In this analysis minimum variance is 0.3 for the DSA algorithm; compared to other algorithms DSA is consistent.

In different bit length DSA is consistent for single character input.

2) Line wise:

- 512 bit length

SAMPLE	RSA	DSA	ELGAMAL
1	2	2	1
2	1	2	2
3	1	2	2
4	1	2	2
5	1	3	2
MEAN	**1.2**	**2.2**	**1.8**

VARIANCE	0.2	0.2	0.2

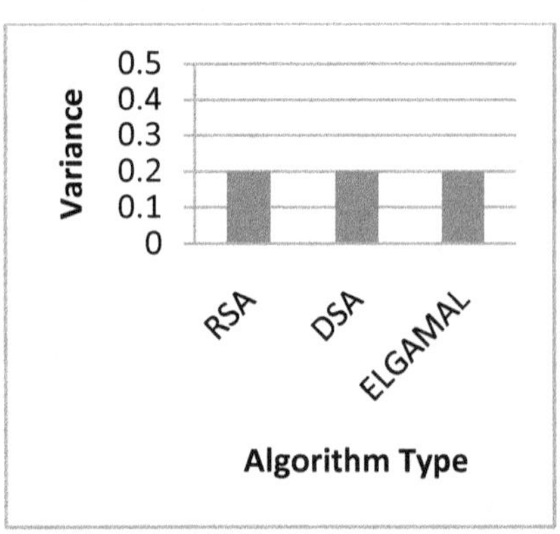

Figure 3.4

In this analysis variance is similar for (i.e 0.2) all algorithms. All algorithms are consistent.

- 1024 bit length

SAMPLE	RSA	DSA	ELGAMAL
1	3	2	5
2	5	3	5
3	6	2	4
4	4	2	2
5	2	2	5
MEAN	**4**	**2.2**	**4.2**
VARIANCE	**2.5**	**0.2**	**1.7**

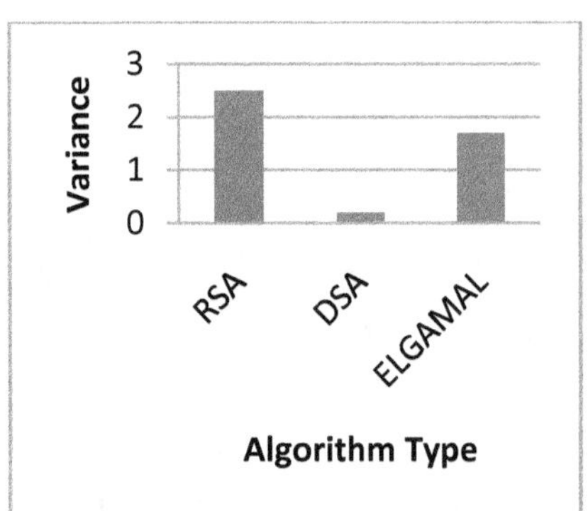

Figure 3.5

In this analysis minimum variance is 0.2 for the DSA algorithm; compared to other algorithms DSA is consistent.

- 2048 bit length

SAMPLE	RSA	DSA	ELGAMAL
1	14	2	12
2	28	3	42
3	30	2	30
4	10	2	20
5	49	3	23

MEAN	26.2	2.4	25.4
VARIANCE	237.2	0.3	127.8

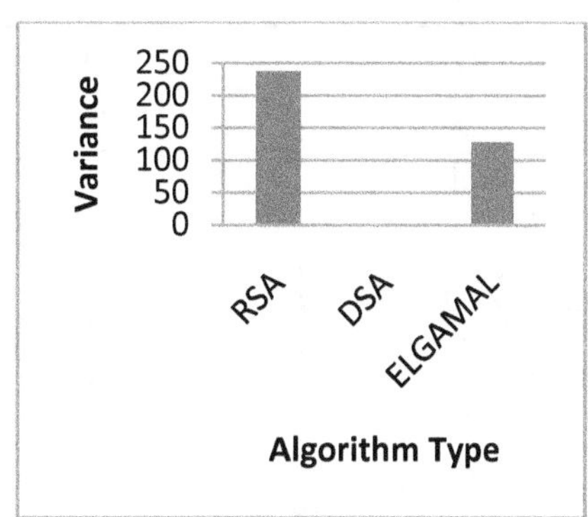

Figure 3.6

In this analysis minimum variance is 0.3 for the DSA algorithm; compared to other algorithms DSA is consistent.

For bit length 512 all algorithms are consistent but for bit length 1024 and 2048 DSA is consistent

3) **Paragraph wise**:
   - 512 bit length

SAMPLE	RSA	DSA	ELGAMAL
1	2	3	1
2	1	3	3
3	1	3	2
4	1	2	2
5	1	2	2
MEAN	1.2	2.6	2
VARIANCE	0.2	0.3	0.5

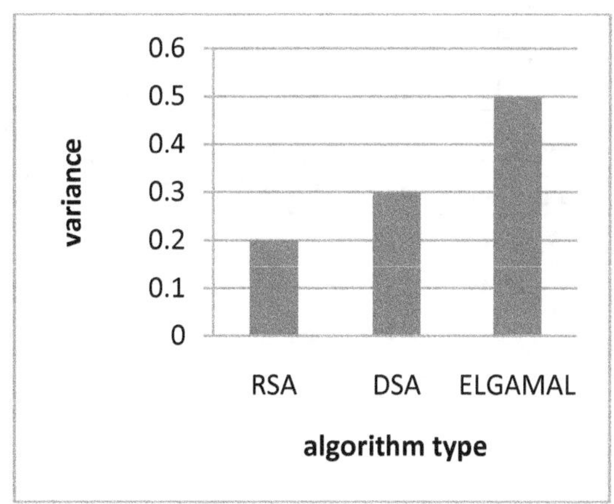

Figure 3.7

In this analysis minimum variance is 0.2 for the RSA algorithm; compared to other algorithms RSA is consistent

- 1024 bit length

SAMPLE	RSA	DSA	ELGAMAL
1	4	2	4
2	4	3	4
3	3	3	5
4	3	3	5
5	3	3	6
MEAN	**3.4**	**2.8**	**4.8**
VARIANCE	**0.3**	**0.2**	**0.7**

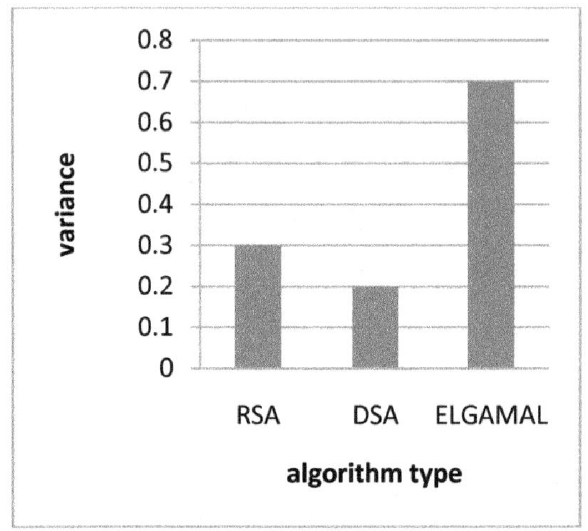

Figure 3.8

In this analysis minimum variance is 0.2 for the DSA algorithm; compared to other algorithms DSA is consistent

- 2048 bit length

SAMPLE	RSA	DSA	ELGAMAL
1	8	3	28
2	73	2	22
3	23	3	28
4	27	3	39
5	11	2	37
MEAN	**28.4**	**2.6**	**30.8**
VARIANCE	**684.8**	**0.3**	**49.7**

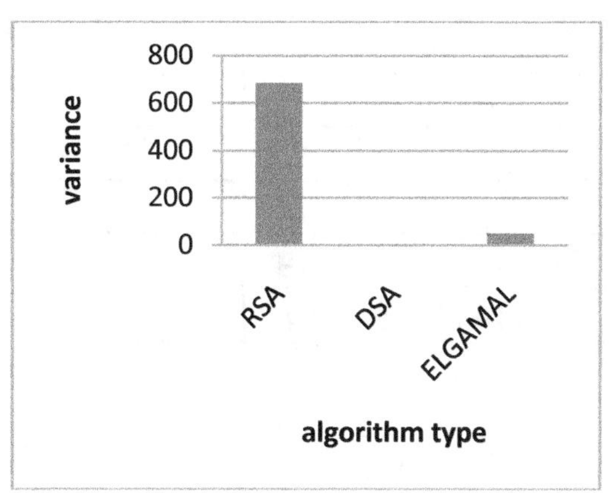

Figure 3.9

In this analysis minimum variance is 0.3 for the DSA algorithm; compared to other algorithms DSA is consistent

Bit length 1024 and 2048 DSA is consistent and RSA is most inconsistent

Windows 7

1) **Character wise**
   - 512 bit length

SAMPLE	RSA	DSA	ELGAMAL
1	3	2	4
2	2	2	2
3	2	3	2
4	2	2	2
5	2	3	2
MEAN	**2.2**	**2.4**	**2.4**
VARIANCE	**0.2**	**0.3**	**0.8**

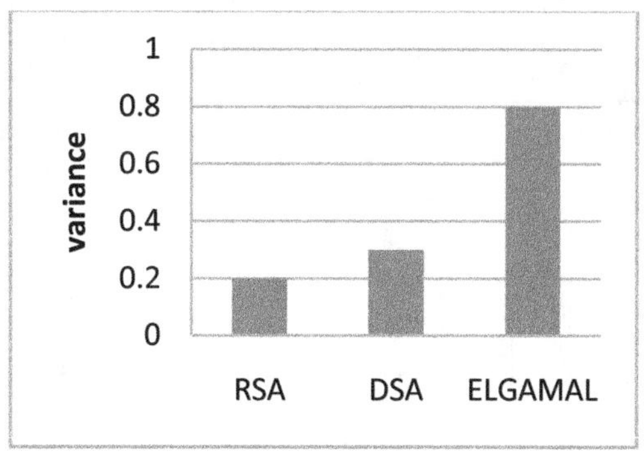

Figure 3.10

In this analysis minimum variance is 0.2 for the DSA algorithm; compared to other algorithms DSA is consistent.

   - 1024 bit length

SAMPLE	RSA	DSA	ELGAMAL
1	7	2	6
2	4	3	4

21

3	3	3	3
4	3	2	7
5	5	2	7
MEAN	**4.4**	**2.4**	**5.4**
VARIANCE	**2.8**	**0.3**	**3.3**

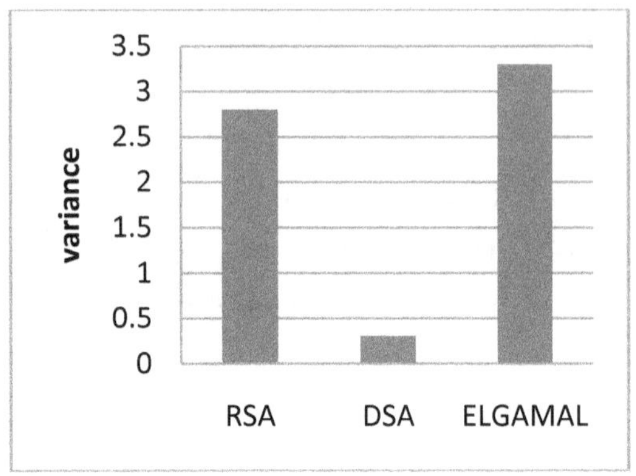

Figure 3.11

In this analysis minimum variance is 0.3 for the DSA algorithm; compared to other algorithms DSA is consistent.

- 2048 bit length

SAMPLE	RSA	DSA	ELGAMAL
1	35	2	57
2	28	2	83
3	44	3	27
4	23	3	13
5	12	2	100
MEAN	**28.4**	**2.4**	**56**
VARIANCE	**146.3**	**0.3**	**1339**

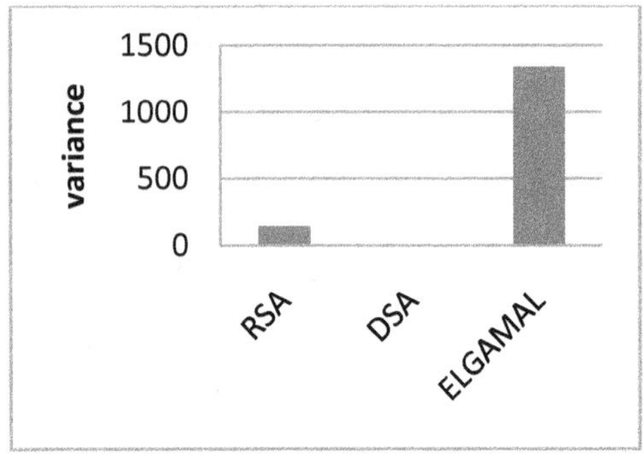

Figure 3.12

In this analysis minimum variance is zero for the 0.3 algorithm; compared to other algorithms DSA is consistent.

Bit length 512, 1024 and 2048 Elgamal algorithm most inconsistent and bit length 512 RSA is consistent then 1024 and 2048 DSA is consistent

2) Line wise
- 512 bit length

SAMPLE	RSA	DSA	ELGAMAL
1	2	2	2
2	2	3	3
3	2	3	2
4	2	2	3
5	2	2	2
MEAN	**2**	**2.4**	**2.4**
VARIANCE	**0**	**0.3**	**0.3**

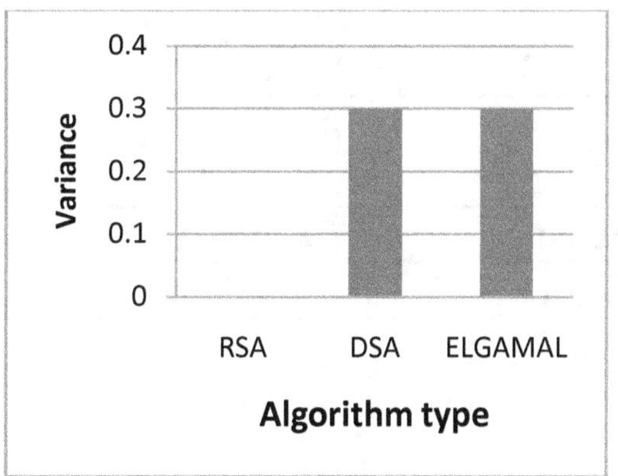

Figure 3.13

In this analysis minimum variance is zero for the RSA algorithm; compared to other algorithms RSA is consistent fig-3.13

- 1024 bit length

SAMPLE	RSA	DSA	ELGAMAL
1	4	2	8
2	4	3	5
3	5	2	3
4	4	2	5
5	6	2	4
MEAN	**4.6**	**2.2**	**5**
VARIANCE	**0.8**	**0.2**	**3.5**

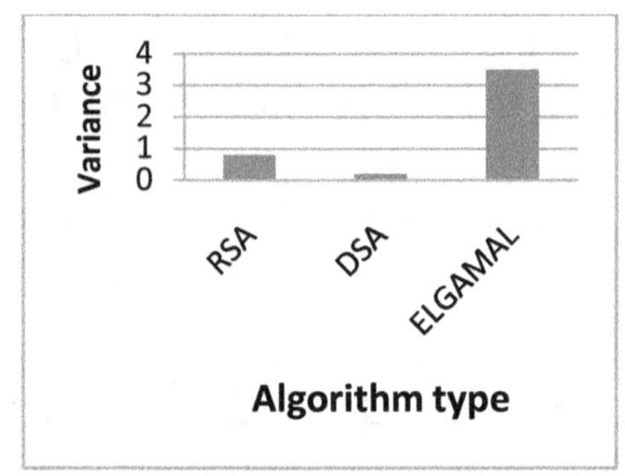

Figure 3.14

In this analysis minimum variance is 0.2 for the DSA algorithm; compared to other algorithms DSA is consistent

- 2048 bit length

SAMPLE	RSA	DSA	ELGAMAL
1	29	3	29
2	17	3	33
3	21	2	32
4	45	2	18
5	24	3	20
MEAN	**27.2**	**2.6**	**26.4**
VARIANCE	**118.2**	**0.3**	**48.3**

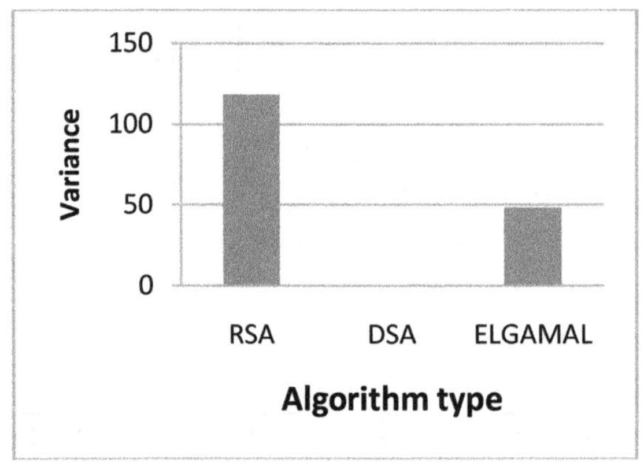

Figure 3.15

In this analysis minimum variance is 0.3 for the DSA algorithm; compared to other algorithms DSA is consistent in fig-3.15
Bit length 512 RSA is consistent and bit length 1024, 2048 DSA is consistent

3) Paragraph wise
- 512 bit length

SAMPLE	RSA	DSA	ELGAMAL
1	2	2	2

2	3	2	3
3	3	3	2
4	2	2	3
5	2	2	2
MEAN	**2.4**	**2.2**	**2.4**
VARIANCE	**0.3**	**0.2**	**0.3**

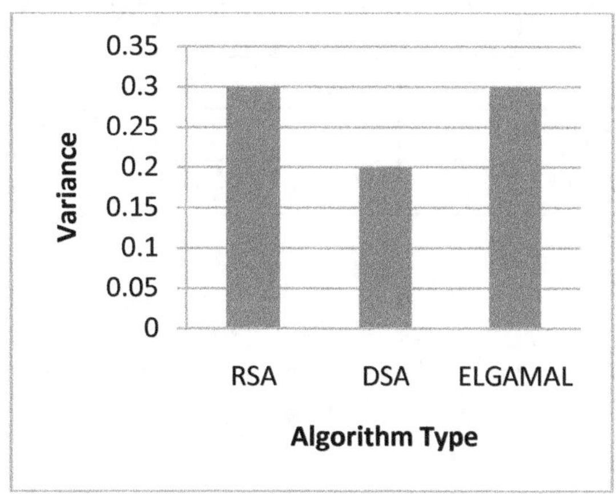

Figure 3.16

In this analysis minimum variance is 0.2 for the DSA algorithm; compared to other algorithms DSA is consistent.

- 1024 bit length

SAMPLE	RSA	DSA	ELGAMAL
1	6	2	5
2	3	3	7
3	3	2	6
4	4	3	4
5	7	3	4
MEAN	**4.6**	**2.6**	**5.2**
VARIANCE	**3.3**	**0.3**	**1.7**

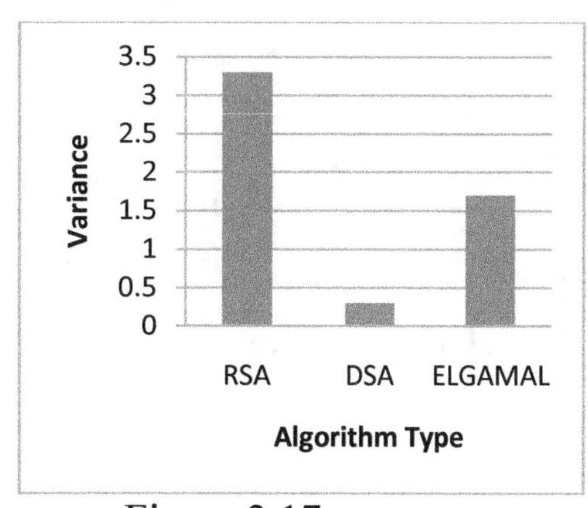

Figure 3.17

In this analysis minimum variance is 0.3 for the DSA algorithm; compared to other algorithms DSA is consistent.

- 2048 bit length

SAMPLE	RSA	DSA	ELGAMAL
1	36	2	34
2	16	3	27
3	10	2	29
4	10	2	27
5	46	3	45
MEAN	**23.6**	**2.4**	**32.4**
VARIANCE	**270.8**	**0.3**	**57.8**

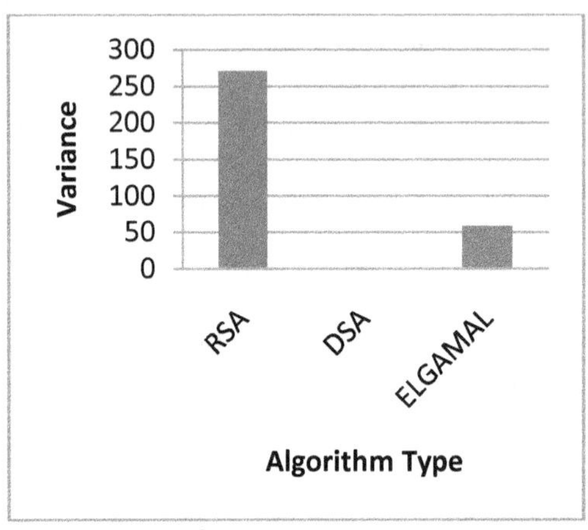

Figure 3.18

In this analysis minimum variance is 0.3 for the DSA algorithm; compared to other algorithms DSA is consistent.

Bit length 512, 1024 2048 RSA and Elgamal are inconsistent but DSA is consistent.

Windows 8

   1) Character wise

- 512 bit length

SAMPLE	RSA	DSA	ELGAMAL
1	2	2	3
2	4	2	2
3	2	2	1
4	1	2	1
5	1	2	2
MEAN	**2**	**2**	**1.8**
VARIANCE	**1.5**	**0**	**0.7**

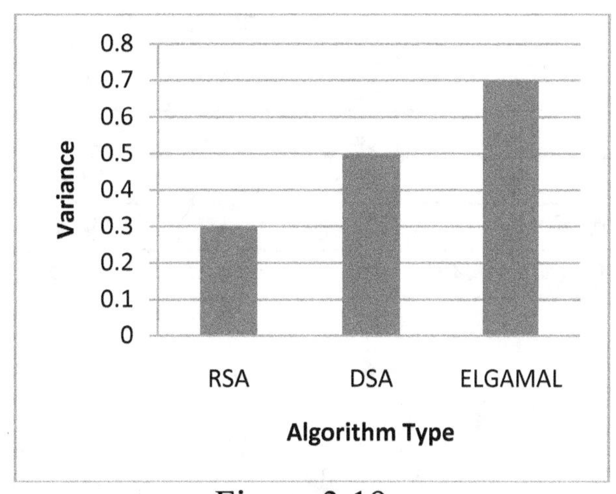

Figure 3.19

In this analysis minimum variance is 0.3 for the DSA algorithm; compared to other algorithms DSA is consistent in fig-3.19.

- 1024 bit length

CHARACTER			
SAMPLE	RSA	DSA	ELGAMAL
1	5	3	7
2	2	2	2
3	2	3	3
4	3	2	4
5	4	2	3
MEAN	**3.2**	**2.4**	**3.8**
VARIANCE	**1.7**	**0.3**	**3.7**

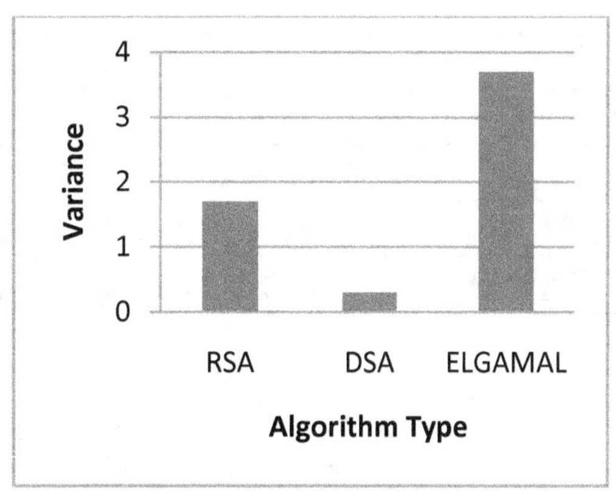

Figure 3.20

In this analysis minimum variance is 0.3 for the DSA algorithm; compared to other algorithms DSA is consistent.

- 2048 bit length

SAMPLE	RSA	DSA	ELGAMAL
1	35	3	13

2	22	3	30
3	33	2	6
4	20	2	30
5	28	3	20
MEAN	**27.6**	**2.6**	**19.8**
VARIANCE	**43.3**	**0.3**	**111.2**

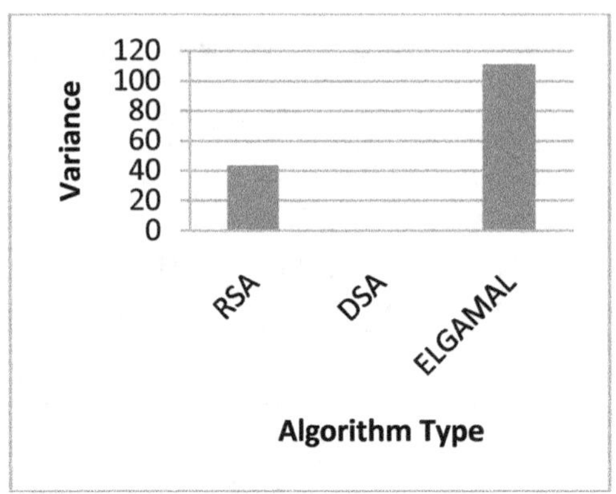

Figure 3.21

In this analysis minimum variance is 0.3 for the DSA algorithm; compared to other algorithms DSA is consistent.

2) Line wise
- 512 bit length

SAMPLE	RSA	DSA	ELGAMAL
1	2	1	2
2	2	3	2
3	1	2	3
4	1	2	3
5	2	3	3
MEAN	**1.6**	**2.2**	**2.6**
VARIANCE	**0.3**	**0.7**	**0.3**

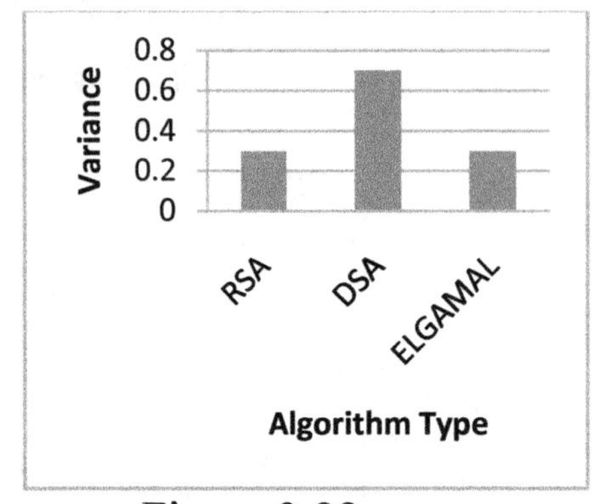

Figure 3.22

In this analysis minimum variance is 0.3 for the RSA and ELGAMAL algorithms; compared to other algorithm RSA and ELGAMAL is consistent.

- 1024 bit length

SAMPLE	RSA	DSA	ELGAMAL
1	3	3	5
2	3	1	3
3	4	3	2
4	2	2	4
5	2	3	2
MEAN	**2.8**	**2.4**	**3.2**
VARIANCE	**0.7**	**0.8**	**1.7**

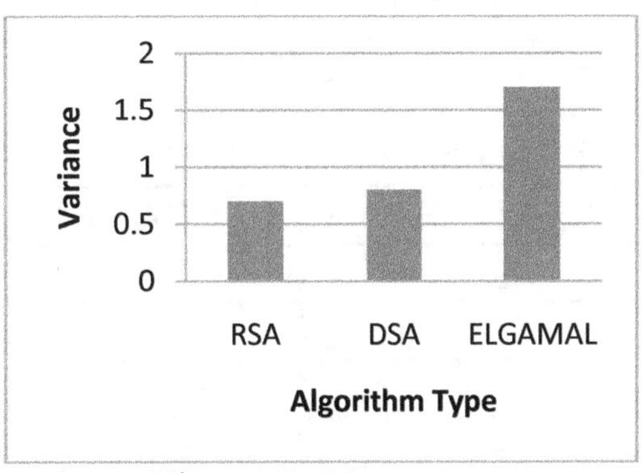

Figure 3.23

In this analysis minimum variance is 0.7 for the RSA algorithm; compared to other algorithms RSA is consistent.

- 2048 bit length

SAMPLE	RSA	DSA	ELGAMAL
1	40	3	18
2	13	2	13
3	38	3	19
4	30	2	38
5	32	3	23
MEAN	**30.6**	**2.6**	**22.2**
VARIANCE	**113.8**	**0.3**	**90.7**

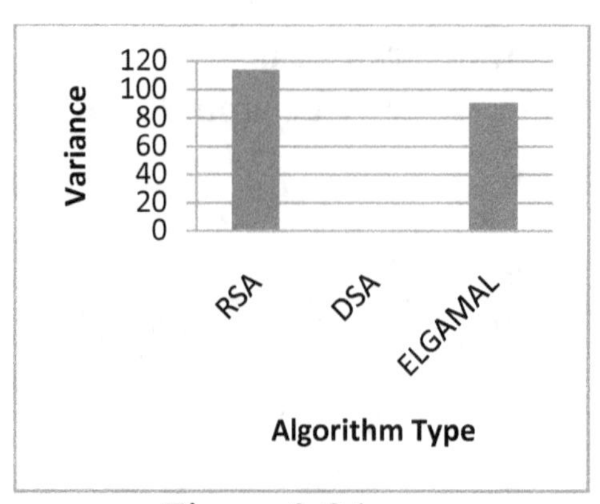

Figure 3.24

In this analysis minimum variance is 0.3 for the DSA algorithm; compared to other algorithms DSA is consistent.

Bit length 512 DSA is inconsistent but bit length 1024 and 2048 DSA is consistent

3) Paragraph wise
- 512 bit length

SAMPLE	RSA	DSA	ELGAMAL
1	1	3	2
2	2	3	3
3	2	2	2
4	2	2	2
5	3	1	2
MEAN	**2**	**2.2**	**2.2**
VARIANCE	**0.5**	**0.7**	**0.2**

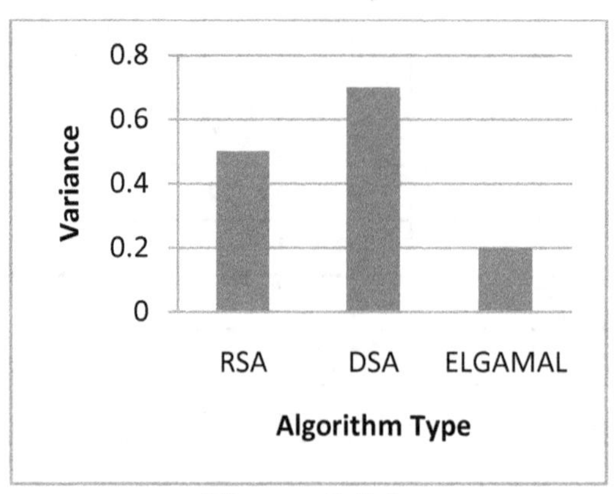

Figure 3.25

In this analysis minimum variance is 0.2 for the ELGAMAL algorithm; compared to other algorithms ELGAMAL is consistent.

- 1024 bit length

SAMPLE	RSA	DSA	ELGAMAL
1	3	3	6
2	2	3	3
3	3	2	4
4	2	2	3
5	5	3	4
MEAN	**3**	**2.6**	**4**
VARIANCE	**1.5**	**0.3**	**1.5**

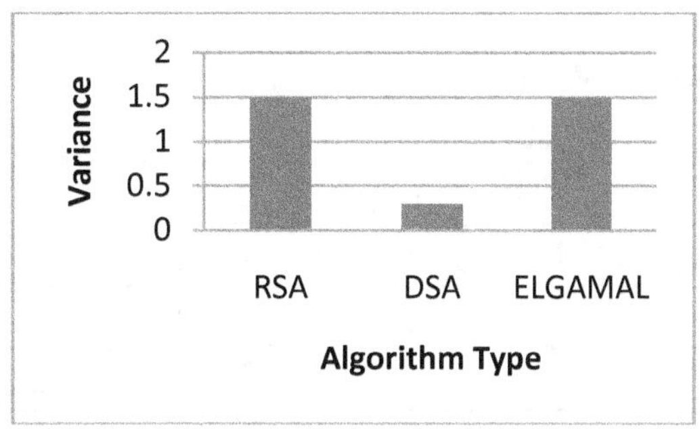

Figure 3.26

In this analysis minimum variance is 0.3 for the DSA algorithm; compared to other algorithms DSA is consistent.

- 2048 bit length

SAMPLE	RSA	DSA	ELGAMAL
1	46	3	24
2	39	3	20
3	40	3	40
4	38	2	39
5	38	2	28
MEAN	**40.2**	**2.6**	**30.2**
VARIANCE	**11.2**	**0.3**	**80.2**

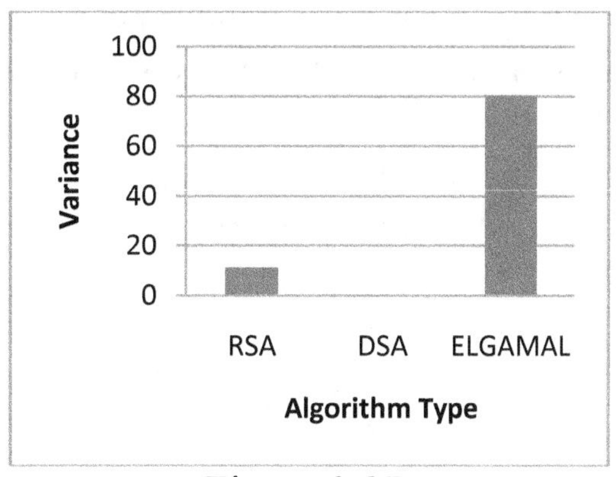

Figure 3.27

In this analysis minimum variance is 0.3 for the DSA algorithm; compared to other algorithms DSA is consistent.

Bi length 512 RSA, DSA are inconsistent and bit length 1024, 2048 DSA is consistent

3.4 Analysis of Correlation between algorithms

There may some kind of relations between various algorithms like DSA, RSA and ELGAMAL. We have analyzed and found correlation coefficient between algorithms

Window XP

   1) Character wise

      • 512 bit length

	1	2	3
SAMPLE	RSA	DSA	ELGAMAL
1	2	2	3
2	4	2	2
3	2	2	1
4	1	2	1
5	1	2	2
r12=	**NOT POSSIBLE**		
r23=	**NOT POSSIBLE**		
r13=	**0.24**		

Table-3.1

Shows that,

Correlation co-efficient of RSA and DSA = NOT POSSIBLE (Divisible by zero)

Correlation co-efficient of DSA and ELGAMAL = NOT POSSIBLE (Divisible by zero)

Correlation co-efficient of RSA and ELGAMAL =0.24

•   It is not possible to calculate correlation coefficient of DSA algorithm with others because all observation of DSA is same so variance of DSA is zero.

•   Correlation coefficient between RSA and Elgamal is 0.24 shows that response time of RSA is increases, responses time of Elgamal is also increases.

- 1024 bit length

	1	2	3
SAMPLE	RSA	DSA	ELGAMAL
1	3	2	2
2	5	2	4
3	3	2	3
4	2	3	2
5	4	2	2
r12=	**-0.69**		
r23=	**-0.38**		
r13=	**0.69**		

Table-3.2

Shows that,

    Correlation co-efficient of RSA and DSA = -0.69

    Correlation co-efficient of DSA and ELGAMAL = -0.38

    Correlation co-efficient of RSA and ELGAMAL =0.69

- Correlation coefficient between RSA and Elgamal is 0.69 shows that response time of RSA is increases, responses time of Elgamal is also increases.
- Correlation coefficient of RSA-DSA and DSA-ELGAMAL algorithms observation are Negative.

  - 2048 bit length

	1	2	3
SAMPLE	RSA	DSA	ELGAMAL
1	57	2	22
2	11	1	19
3	75	2	35
4	28	1	52
5	17	2	14
r12=	**0.60**		
r23=	**-0.42**		
r13=	**0.26**		

Table-3.3

Shows that,

    Correlation co-efficient of RSA and DSA = 0.60

    Correlation co-efficient of DSA and ELGAMAL =-0.42

    Correlation co-efficient of RSA and ELGAMAL =0.26

- Correlation coefficient between RSA and DSA is 0.26 shows that response time of RSA is increases, responses time of DSA is also increases.
- Correlation coefficient of DSA-ELGAMAL algorithms observation is Negative.

2) Line wise
- 512 bit length

	1	2	3
SAMPLE	RSA	DSA	ELGAMAL
1	2	2	1
2	1	2	2
3	1	2	2
4	1	2	2
5	1	3	2
r12=	**-0.25**		
r23=	**0.25**		
r13=	**-1.00**		

Table-3.4

Shows that,

Correlation co-efficient of RSA and DSA = -0.25

Correlation co-efficient of DSA and ELGAMAL =- 0.25

Correlation co-efficient of RSA and ELGAMAL =- 1.00

- Correlation coefficient between DSA and ELGAMAL is 0.24 shows that response time of DSA is increases, responses time of EJGAMAL is also increases.
- Correlation coefficient of RSA-DSA and DSA-ELGAMAL algorithms observation are Negative.
  - 1024 bit length

	1	2	3
SAMPLE	RSA	DSA	ELGAMAL
1	3	2	5
2	5	3	5
3	6	2	4
4	4	2	2
5	2	2	5
r12=	**0.35**		
r23=	**0.34**		
r13=	**-0.24**		

Table-3.5

Show That,

    Correlation co-efficient of RSA and DSA = 0.35

    Correlation co-efficient of DSA and ELGAMAL =0.34

    Correlation co-efficient of RSA and ELGAMAL =--0.24

- Correlation coefficient between DSA and ELGAMAL is 0.34 shows that response time of DSA is increases, responses time of ELGAMAL is also increases.
- Correlation coefficient of RSA-ELGAMAL algorithms observation is Negative.
  - 2048 bit length

	1	2	3
SAMPLE	RSA	DSA	ELGAMAL
1	14	2	12
2	28	3	42
3	30	2	30
4	10	2	20
5	49	3	23
r12=	**0.73**		
r23=	**0.57**		
r13=	**0.35**		

Table-3.6

Shows that,

    Correlation co-efficient of RSA and DSA = 0.73

    Correlation co-efficient of DSA and ELGAMAL = 0.57

    Correlation co-efficient of RSA and ELGAMAL = 0.35

- Correlation coefficient between RSA and ELGAMAL is 0.35 shows that response time of RSA is increases, responses time of ELGAMAL is also increases.
- Correlation coefficient of all algorithms observation is positive.

3) Paragraph wise
  - 512 bit length

	1	2	3
SAMPLE	RSA	DSA	ELGAMAL
1	2	3	1
2	1	3	3
3	1	3	2
4	1	2	2
5	1	2	2

r12=	0.41
r23=	0.00
r13=	-0.79

Table-3.7

Shows that,

Correlation co-efficient of RSA and DSA = 0.41

Correlation co-efficient of DSA and ELGAMAL = 0.00

Correlation co-efficient of RSA and ELGAMAL = -0.79

- Correlation coefficient between DSA and ELGAMAL is 0 shows that response time of DSA is increases, responses time of ELGAMAL is also increases.
- Correlation coefficient of RSA-ELGAMAL algorithms observation is Negative.
  - 1024 bit length

	1	2	3
SAMPLE	RSA	DSA	ELGAMAL
1	4	2	4
2	4	3	4
3	3	3	5
4	3	3	5
5	3	3	6
r12=	-0.61		
r23=	0.53		
r13=	-0.87		

Table-3.8

Shows that,

Correlation co-efficient of RSA and DSA = -0.61

Correlation co-efficient of DSA and ELGAMAL = 0.53

Correlation co-efficient of RSA and ELGAMAL = -0.87

- Correlation coefficient between DSA and ELGAMAL is 0.53 shows that response time of RSA is increases, responses time of elgamal is also increases.
- Correlation coefficient of RSA-DSA and RSA-ELGAMAL algorithms observation is Negative.

- 2048 bit length

	1	2	3
SAMPLE	RSA	DSA	ELGAMAL
1	8	3	28
2	73	2	22
3	23	3	28
4	27	3	39
5	11	2	37
r12=	**-0.47**		
r23=	**0.17**		
r13=	**-0.60**		

Table-3.9

Shows that,

Correlation co-efficient of RSA and DSA = -0.47

Correlation co-efficient of DSA and ELGAMAL = 0.17

Correlation co-efficient of RSA and ELGAMAL = -0.60

- Correlation coefficient between DSA and ELGAMAL is 0.17 shows that response time of DSA is increases, responses time of ELGAMAL is also increases.
- Correlation coefficient of RSA-DSA and RSA-ELGAMAL algorithms observation is Negative.

Window 7

1) Character wise

- 512 bit length

	1	2	3
SAMPLE	RSA	DSA	ELGAMAL
1	3	2	4
2	2	2	2
3	2	3	2
4	2	2	2
5	2	3	2
r12	**-0.41**		
r23	**-0.41**		
r13	**1.00**		

Table-3.10

Shows that,

Correlation co-efficient of RSA and DSA = -0.41

Correlation co-efficient of DSA and ELGAMAL = - 0.41

Correlation co-efficient of RSA and ELGAMAL = 1.00

- Correlation coefficient between RSA and ELGAMAL is 1.00 shows that response time of RSA is increases, responses time of ELGAMAL is also increases.
- Correlation coefficient of RSA-DSA and DSA-ELGAMAL algorithms observation is Negative.
  - 1024 bit length

	1	2	3
SAMPLE	RSA	DSA	ELGAMAL
1	7	2	6
2	4	3	4
3	3	3	3
4	3	2	7
5	5	2	7
r12	**-0.49**		
r23	**-0.95**		
r13	**0.35**		

Table-3.11

Shows that,

Correlation co-efficient of RSA and DSA = -0.49

Correlation co-efficient of DSA and ELGAMAL = - 0.95

Correlation co-efficient of RSA and ELGAMAL = 0.35

- Correlation coefficient between RSA and ELGAMAL is 0.35 shows that response time of RSA is increases, responses time of DSA is also increases.
- Correlation coefficient of RSA-DSA and DSA-ELGAMAL algorithms observation is Negative.
  - 2048 bit length

	1	2	3
SAMPLE	RSA	DSA	ELGAMAL
1	35	2	57
2	28	2	83
3	44	3	27
4	23	3	13
5	12	2	100
r12	**-0.92**		

| r23 | -0.90 |
| r13 | -0.53 |

Table-3.12

Shows that,

Correlation co-efficient of RSA and DSA = -0.92

Correlation co-efficient of DSA and ELGAMAL =--0.90

Correlation co-efficient of RSA and ELGAMAL = -0.53

- Correlation coefficient of all algorithms observation is Negative.

2) Line wise

- 512 bit length

	1	2	3
SAMPLE	RSA	DSA	ELGAMAL
1	2	2	2
2	2	3	3
3	2	3	2
4	2	2	3
5	2	2	2
r12	**NOT POSSIBLE**		
r23	**0.17**		
r13	**NOT POSSIBLE**		

Table-3.13

Shows that,

Correlation co-efficient of RSA and DSA = NOT POSSIBLE   (Divisible by Zero)

Correlation co-efficient of DSA and ELGAMAL =- 0.17

Correlation co-efficient of RSA and ELGAMAL = NOT POSSIBLE

- Correlation coefficient between DSA and ELGAMAL is 0.17 shows that response time of DSA is increases, responses time of ELGAMAL is also increases.

- It is not possible to calculate Correlation coefficient of RSA algorithm with others, because all observation of RSA is same so variance of RSA is zero.

- 1024 bit length

	1	2	3
SAMPLE	RSA	DSA	ELGAMAL
1	4	2	8
2	4	3	5
3	5	2	3

4	4	2	5
5	6	2	4
r12	**-0.38**		
r23	**0.00**		
r13	**-0.60**		

Table-3.14

Shows that,

      Correlation co-efficient of RSA and DSA = -0.38

      Correlation co-efficient of DSA and ELGAMAL = 0.00

      Correlation co-efficient of RSA and ELGAMAL = -0.60

- Correlation coefficient of DSA-ELGAMAL algorithm with each other, because all observation of DSA is same so variance of ELGAMAL is zero.
- Correlation coefficient between RSA-DSA and RSA-ELGAMAL is negative.

- 2048 bit length

	1	2	3
SAMPLE	RSA	DSA	ELGAMAL
1	29	3	29
2	17	3	33
3	21	2	32
4	45	2	18
5	24	3	20
r12	**-0.49**		
r23	**0.18**		
r13	**-0.75**		

Table-3.15

Shows that,

      Correlation co-efficient of RSA and DSA = -0.49

      Correlation co-efficient of DSA and ELGAMAL = 0.18

      Correlation co-efficient of RSA and ELGAMAL = -0.75

- Correlation coefficient between DSA and ELGAMAL is 0.18 shows that response time of DSA is increases, responses time of ELGAMAL is also increases.
- Correlation coefficient of RSA-DSA and RSA-ELGAMAL algorithms observation is Negative

3) Paragraph wise

- 512 bit length

	1	2	3
SAMPLE	RSA	DSA	ELGAMAL
1	2	2	2
2	3	2	3
3	3	3	2
4	2	2	3
5	2	2	2
r12	**0.61**		
r23	**-0.41**		
r13	**0.17**		

Table-3.16

Shows that,

Correlation co-efficient of RSA and DSA = 0.61

Correlation co-efficient of DSA and ELGAMAL = - 0.41

Correlation co-efficient of RSA and ELGAMAL = 0.17

- Correlation coefficient between DSA and ELGAMAL is 0.18 shows that response time of DSA is increases, responses time of ELGAMAL is also increases.
- Correlation coefficient of RSA-DSA and RSA-ELGAMAL algorithms observation is Negative

- 1024 bit length

	1	2	3
SAMPLE	RSA	DSA	ELGAMAL
1	6	2	5
2	3	3	7
3	3	2	6
4	4	3	4
5	7	3	4
r12	**0.05**		
r23	**-0.21**		
r13	**-0.70**		

Table-3.17

Shows that,

Correlation co-efficient of RSA and DSA = 0.05

Correlation co-efficient of DSA and ELGAMAL = - 0.21

Correlation co-efficient of RSA and ELGAMAL = 0.70

- Correlation coefficient between RSA and DSA is 0.05 shows that response time of RSA is increases, responses time of DSA is also increases.
- Correlation coefficient of DSA-ELGAMAL and RSA-ELGAMAL algorithms observation is Negative

- 2048 bit length

	1	2	3
SAMPLE	RSA	DSA	ELGAMAL
1	36	2	34
2	16	3	27
3	10	2	29
4	10	2	27
5	46	3	45
r12	**0.41**		
r23	**0.43**		
r13	**0.92**		

Table-3.18

Shows that,

Correlation co-efficient of RSA and DSA = 0.41

Correlation co-efficient of DSA and ELGAMAL = 0.43

Correlation co-efficient of RSA and ELGAMAL = 0.92

- Correlation coefficient between RSA and DSA is 0.41 shows that response time of RSA is increases, responses time of DSA is also increases.
- Correlation coefficient of DSA-ELGAMAL and RSA-ELGAMAL algorithms observation is Positive.

Window 8

1) Character wise

- 512 bit length

	1	2	3
SAMPLE	RSA	DSA	ELGAMAL
1	2	3	3
2	2	2	2
3	3	2	2
4	3	2	1
5	2	1	1
r12	**0.00**		
r23	**0.85**		
r13	**-0.33**		

Table-3.19

Shows that,

Correlation co-efficient of RSA and DSA = 0.00

Correlation co-efficient of DSA and ELGAMAL = 0.85

Correlation co-efficient of RSA and ELGAMAL = -0.33

- Correlation coefficient between RSA and DSA is 0.00 shows that response time of RSA is increases, responses time of DSA is also increases.
- Correlation coefficient of DSA-ELGAMAL is positive and RSA-ELGAMAL algorithms observation is negative.

- 1024 bit length

	1	2	3
SAMPLE	RSA	DSA	ELGAMAL
1	5	3	7
2	2	2	2
3	2	3	3
4	3	2	4
5	4	2	3
r12	**0.21**		
r23	**0.57**		
r13	**0.82**		

Table-3.20

Shows that,

Correlation co-efficient of RSA and DSA = 0.21

Correlation co-efficient of DSA and ELGAMAL = 0.57

Correlation co-efficient of RSA and ELGAMAL = 0.82

- Correlation coefficient between RSA and DSA is 0.21 shows that response time of RSA is increases, responses time of DSA is also increases.
- Correlation coefficient of DSA-ELGAMAL and RSA-ELGAMAL algorithms observation is Positive
  - 2048 bit length

	1	2	3
SAMPLE	RSA	DSA	ELGAMAL
1	35	3	13
2	22	3	30
3	33	2	6
4	20	2	30
5	28	3	20
r12	**0.15**		
r23	**0.16**		
r13	**-0.93**		

Table-3.21

Shows that,

Correlation co-efficient of RSA and DSA = 0.15Correlation co-efficient of DSA and ELGAMAL = 0.16Correlation co-efficient of RSA and ELGAMAL = -0.93

- Correlation coefficient between RSA and DSA is 0.15 shows that response time of RSA is increases, responses time of DSA is also increases.
- Correlation coefficient of DSA-ELGAMAL is positive and RSA-ELGAMAL algorithms observation is negative.

2) Line wise
  - 512 bit length

	1	2	3
SAMPLE	RSA	DSA	ELGAMAL
1	2	1	2
2	2	3	2
3	1	2	3
4	1	2	3
5	2	3	3
r12	**0.22**		
r23	**0.22**		
r13	**-0.67**		

Table-3.22

Shows that,

Correlation co-efficient of RSA and DSA = 0.22Correlation co-efficient of DSA and ELGAMAL = 0.22Correlation co-efficient of RSA and ELGAMAL = -0.67

- Correlation coefficient between RSA-DSA and DSA-ELGAMAL is 0.22 shows that response time of RSA is increases, responses time of DSA is also increases.
- Correlation coefficient of RSA-ELGAMAL algorithms observation is Positive.
  - 1024 bit length

	1	2	3
SAMPLE	RSA	DSA	ELGAMAL
1	3	3	5
2	3	1	3
3	4	3	2
4	2	2	4
5	2	3	2
r12	**0.13**		
r23	**-0.09**		
r13	**-0.18**		

Table-3.23

Shows that,

Correlation co-efficient of RSA and DSA = 0.13Correlation co-efficient of DSA and ELGAMAL = -0.09Correlation co-efficient of RSA and ELGAMAL = -0.18

- Correlation coefficient between RSA-DSA is 0.11 shows that response time of RSA is increases, responses time of DSA is also increases.
- Correlation coefficient of RSA-ELGAMAL and RSA-ELGAMAL algorithms observation is Negative.
  - 2048 bit length

	1	2	3
SAMPLE	RSA	DSA	ELGAMAL
1	40	3	18
2	13	2	13
3	38	3	19
4	30	2	38
5	32	3	23
r12	**0.78**		
r23	**-0.32**		
r13	**0.22**		

Table-3.24

Shows that,

Correlation co-efficient of RSA and DSA = 0.78

Correlation co-efficient of DSA and ELGAMAL = - 0.32

Correlation co-efficient of RSA and ELGAMAL = 0.22

- Correlation coefficient between RSA-ELGAMAL is 0.22 shows that response time of RSA is increases, responses time of ELGAMAL is also increases.
- Correlation coefficient of RSA-DSA is Positive and DSA-ELGAMAL algorithms observation is Negative

3) Paragraph wise

- 512 bit length

	1	2	3
SAMPLE	RSA	DSA	ELGAMAL
1	1	3	2
2	2	3	3
3	2	2	2
4	2	2	2
5	3	1	2
r12	**-0.85**		
r23	**0.53**		
r13	**0.00**		

Table-3.25

Shows that,

Correlation co-efficient of RSA and DSA = -0.85

Correlation co-efficient of DSA and ELGAMAL = 0.53

Correlation co-efficient of RSA and ELGAMAL = 0.00

- Correlation coefficient between RSA-ELGAMAL is 0.00 shows that response time of RSA is increases, responses time of ELGAMAL is also increases.
- Correlation coefficient of RSA-DSA is Negative and DSA-ELGAMAL algorithms observation is Positive

- 1024 bit length

	1	2	3
SAMPLE	RSA	DSA	ELGAMAL
1	3	3	6
2	2	3	3
3	3	2	4
4	2	2	3
5	5	3	4
r12	**0.37**		
r23	**0.37**		
r13	**0.33**		

Table-3.26

Shows that,

Correlation co-efficient of RSA and DSA = 0.37

Correlation co-efficient of DSA and ELGAMAL = 0.37Correlation co-efficient of RSA and ELGAMAL = 0.33

- Correlation coefficient between RSA and ELGAMAL is 0.33 shows that response time of RSA is increases, responses time of ELGAMAL is also increases.
- Correlation coefficient of RSA-DSA and DSA-ELGAMAL algorithms observation is Positive.

- 2048 bit length

	1	2	3
SAMPLE	RSA	DSA	ELGAMAL
1	46	3	24
2	39	3	20
3	40	3	40
4	38	2	39
5	38	2	28
r12	**0.60**		
r23	**-0.34**		
r13	**-0.34**		

Table-3.27

Shows that,

Correlation co-efficient of RSA and DSA = 0.60Correlation co-efficient of DSA and ELGAMAL = -0.34Correlation co-efficient of RSA and ELGAMAL = -0.34

- Correlation coefficient between RSA and DSA is 0.60 shows that response time of RSA is increases, responses time of ELGAMAL is also increases.

- Correlation coefficient of DSA-ELGAMAL and RSA-ELGAMAL algorithms observation is Negative.

3.5 ANALYSIS OF VARIANCE TABLE

WINDOWS XP (CHARACTER)		
ALGORITHM	BIT LENGTH	
	2048	1024	512
RSA	749.8	1.3	1.5
DSA	0.3	0.2	0
ELGAMAL	234.3	0.8	0.7

Table-3.28

This data shows that for bit length 2048, variance of RSA and ELGAMAL is very high

WINDOWS XP (LINE)		
ALGORITHM	BIT LENGTH	
	2048	1024	512
RSA	237.2	2.5	0.2
DSA	0.3	0.2	0.2
ELGAMAL	127.8	1.7	0.2

Table-3.29

This data shows that for bit length 2048, variance of RSA and ELGAMAL is very high

WINDOWS XP (PARAGRAPH)		
ALGORITHM	BIT LENGTH	
	2048	1024	512
RSA	684.8	0.3	0.2
DSA	0.3	0.2	0.3
ELGAMAL	49.7	0.7	0.5

Table-3.30

This data shows that for bit length 2048, variance of RSA and ELGAMAL is very high

WINDOWS 7 (CHARACTER)		
ALGORITHM	BIT LENGTH	
	2048	1024	512
RSA	146.3	2.8	0.2
DSA	0.3	0.3	0.3
ELGAMAL	1339	3.3	0.8

Table-3.31

This data shows that for bit length 2048, variance of RSA and ELGAMAL is very high

WINDOWS 7 (LINE)			
ALGORITHM	BIT LENGTH		
	2048	1024	512
RSA	118.2	0.8	0
DSA	0.3	0.2	0.3
ELGAMAL	48.3	3.5	0.3

Table-3.32

This data shows that for bit length 2048, variance of RSA and ELGAMAL is very high

WINDOWS 7 (PARAGRAPH)			
ALGORITHM	BIT LENGTH		
	2048	1024	512
RSA	270.8	3.3	0.3
DSA	0.3	0.3	0.2
ELGAMAL	57.8	1.7	0.3

Table-3.33

This data shows that for bit length 2048, variance of RSA and ELGAMAL is very high

WINDOWS 8 (CHARACTER)			
ALGORITHM	BIT LENGTH		
	2048	1024	512
RSA	43.3	1.7	0.3
DSA	0.3	0.3	0.5
ELGAMAL	111.2	3.7	0.7

Table-3.34

This data shows that for bit length 2048, variance of RSA and ELGAMAL is very high

WINDOWS 8 (LINE)			
ALGORITHM	BIT LENGTH		
	2048	1024	512
RSA	113.8	0.7	0.3
DSA	0.3	0.8	0.7
ELGAMAL	90.7	1.7	0.3

Table-3.35

This data shows that for bit length 2048, variance of RSA and ELGAMAL is very high

WINDOWS 8 (PARAGRAPH)			
ALGORITHM	BIT LENGTH		
	2048	1024	512

	11.2	1.5	0.5
RSA	11.2	1.5	0.5
DSA	0.3	0.3	0.7
ELGAMAL	80.2	1.5	0.2

Table-3.36

This data shows that for bit length 2048, variance of RSA and ELGAMAL is very high

Conclusion

In above analysis describe for bit length 2048 for various operating system with a character, Line and Paragraph, we conclude that variance is very high for RSA and ELGAMAL, variance of DSA algorithm result in all operating system and bit lengths are minimum.

Then bit length 1024 and 512 for various operating system and a character, Line and paragraph, variance of all algorithms are minimum.

3.6 CORRELATION CO-EFFICIENT TABLE

Correlation co-efficient between various algorithms is calculated all three algorithms.

Operating System	TYPE	BITLENGTH	RSA-DSA	DSA-ELGAMAL	RSA-ELGAMAL
WINDOS XP	CHARACTER	2048	0.60	-0.42	0.26
		1024	-0.69	-0.38	0.69
		512	NOT POSSIBLE	0.35	0.24
	LINE	2048	0.73	0.57	0.35
		1024	0.35	0.34	-0.24
		512	-0.25	0.25	-1.00
	PARAGRAPH	2048	-0.47	0.17	-0.60
		1024	-0.61	0.53	-0.87
		512	0.41	0.00	-0.79
WINDOWS 7	CHARACTER	2048	-0.92	-0.90	-0.53
		1024	-0.49	-0.95	0.35
		512	-0.41	-0.41	1.00
	LINE	2048	-0.49	0.18	-0.75
		1024	-0.38	0.00	-0.60
		512	NOT POSSIBLE	0.17	NOT POSSIBLE

	PARAGRAPH	2048	0.41	0.43	0.92
		1024	0.05	-0.21	-0.70
		512	0.61	-0.41	0.17
WIDOWS 8	CHARACTER	2048	0.15	0.16	-0.93
		1024	0.21	0.57	0.82
		512	0.00	0.85	-0.33
	LINE	2048	0.78	-0.32	0.22
		1024	0.13	-0.09	-0.18
		512	0.22	0.22	-0.67
	PARAGRAPH	2048	0.60	-0.34	-0.34
		1024	0.37	0.37	0.33
		512	-0.85	0.53	0.00

Table 3.37:

Result

The positive result indicates that both algorithm correlates and works in same direction.

The negative result indicates that both algorithm does not correlate and works in different direction.

The result that is obtained as NOT POSSIBLE is because the correlation cannot be established between those algorithms because the final data sample obtained between the two algorithms is almost similar and therefore cannot be compared.

Conclusion

- In this analysis for windows 7 bit length 2048 single character, all algorithms are negative correlated, so response time between algorithms is in opposite direction.
- There are positively correlated all algorithms for windows XP, line wise 2048 bit length, windows 7 paragraph wise 2048 bit length , windows 8 character wise and paragraph wise. So response time between algorithms is in same direction.
- Windows 8 with 1024 bit length with character wise and paragraph wise, all algorithms are positive correlated.
- In windows XP and windows 7 for 512 bit length some time it is not possible to find correlation co-efficient (It is indicated in Table no 3.37), because variance of algorithms becomes zero.
- In windows 8 most of times algorithms are positive correlated.
- In windows XP and windows 7 due to zero variance correlated co-efficient could not be calculated. It does not mean it is negative factor

but we consider it is positive sign because these algorithms are very much consistent.

52

Chapter -4

Design, Model & Development of Public Key Algorithm

4.1 RSA Advantage & Limitation

- It is a kind of algorithm that can be used for only data encryption since forty years. It has experienced all kinds of attacks and the test. It has been gradually accepted by the people and is considered to be one of the best public key schemes.

- This algorithm is based on large integers and prime testing; its mathematical basis is the Euler theorem.

- The user should not worry if public key is leaked, but need to consider someone takes another's place by counterfeiting published false public key, so it should be possible to widely publish the right key to public to prevent counterfeiting

- Complexity of the key creation. Because the RSA algorithm is limited by the prime and efficiency of generating primes is relatively low, so it is difficult to achieve a secret once (Internet Data Center, 2011)

- Security needs to be proofed. The RSA security depends on the difficulty of factoring large numbers, but is equivalent to factoring has not been proved theoretically, because there is no proof of cracked RSA will need factorization. If there is an algorithm can fast decompose a large number, so the RSA algorithm's security would be threatened. In addition, the computational ability of the computer to continuously improve, the cost of computer to reduce, the parallel technology of the computer to develop, then attack the RSA algorithm will get huge growth ability

- Slow of the speed. The RSA encryption and decryption algorithm need a lot of calculation and the speed is slowly, compared with the symmetric cryptographic algorithm thousands of times slower. With the development of large number of decomposition technique, key length would increase to ensure safety, so the computation will be greater

In this study is based on fully research and a deep understanding of the principle of tradition RSA algorithm, the RSA algorithm is implemented in Java environment and analyzes the security of RSA algorithm and its disadvantages. On the whole, the RSA algorithm is a good algorithm. But in the application of the RSA algorithm, RSA algorithm also has many problems, such as the public key is correct, the encryption and decryption speed is very slow and the key generation is very troublesome.[16]

4.2 Elgamal Algorithm advantages and disadvantages

- Elgamal has the disadvantage that the ciphertext is twice as long as the plaintext.
- It has the advantage the same plaintext gives a different ciphertext (with near certainty) each time it is encrypted.
- Encryption depends on the keys of the sender, not suitable for secret communication.
- Stronger cryptographic assumption is necessary: Hard to calculate discrete logarithm, even if one selects p, g in a special way, still not broken, risky anyway
- In this algorithm is mostly used to encrypt small amount of data, exchange of small messages or secret keys.

It should also be mentioned that the Elgamal cryptosystem over elliptic curve is suitable to be implemented on many small devices (e.g. smart card) where limited processing power and limited memory capacity exist, this is due to the small number of bits required to perform the encryption and decryption process.

4.3 DSA Advantage and limitation

- DES uses 16 48-bits keys generated from a master 56-bit key (64 bits if we consider also parity bits)
- Weak keys: keys make the same sub-key to be generated in more than one round.
  Result: reduce cipher complexity
- A digital signature algorithm is a public key cryptographic algorithm designed to protect the authenticity of a digital message or document.
- Authentication: identification of the person that signs.
- Integrity of data: every change will be detected.
- Non repudiation: because the author cannot be denied of his work (he created and sent).
- Imposter prevention: Elimination of possibility of committing fraud by an imposter.
- The private key must be kept in a secured manner. The loss of private key can cause severe damage since, anyone who gets the private
  key can use it to send signed messages to the public key holders and
  the public key will recognize these messages as valid and so the receivers will feel that the message was sent by the authentic private
  key holder.

- The process of generation and verification of digital signature requires considerable amount of time. So, for frequent exchange of messages the speed of communication will reduce.
- When the digital signature is not verified by the public key, then the receiver simply marks the message as invalid but he does not know
whether the message was corrupted or the false private key was used.
- For using the digital signature the user has to obtain private and public key, the receiver has to obtain the digital signature certificate also. This requires them to pay additional amount of money.
- Although digital signature provides authenticity, it does not ensure secrecy of the data. To provide the secrecy, some other technique such as encryption and decryption needs to be used.
Though the use of Digital Signature is very powerful way to secure and authenticate a message or document, its advantages are hampered by lost or theft of keys and the use of vulnerable storage facilities. A number of digital signature standard exist which are incompatible with each other and there is a strong need of a standard through which these different methods (keys) can interact.[17]

4.4 Features of suggested model
- Less calculation time for all bit length and different Operating Systems for encryption and decryption
- Convert small and large amount of data in same time.
- Cipher text is not decrypted without secret key.
- Message corrupts when wrong private key is entered.
- Same plaintext generates different cipher text (with near certainty) each time it is encrypted
- ASCII codes are used to establish standard character definitions as well as some standard formatting.
- Complement's method is use for data security.
- Binary Conversation Method for better Security.

4.5 Designing Specification
Security is the important factor in the public network and cryptography plays   important role in this field. Cryptography is very old and secured technique of   information   in   public   network. However, the objective of cryptography is used   not   only   to   provide confidentiality, but also to provide solutions for other   problems: data

integrity, authentication, non-repudiation. Cryptography is the science of devising methods that allow information to be sent in a secure form in such a way that the only person able to retrieve this information is the intended recipient [4]. Cryptography is broadly divided into two categories depending upon the Key; which is defined as the rules used to convert an original text into encrypted text: - Symmetric Key Encryption and Asymmetric Key Encryption. Symmetric Key Encryption uses the same key for encryption and decryption processes. This technique is simple yet powerful but key distribution is the chief problem that needs to be addressed Whereas, Asymmetric Key Encryption use two mathematically associated keys: Public Key & Private Key for encryption. The public key is available to everyone but the data once encrypted by public key of any user can only be decrypted by private key of that particular user.

The process is a bit lengthy and complicated but it enhances the security. Figure 1 is showing simple encryption decryption process formally say its showing cryptography concept.

Basically this Research is proposing a new encryption algorithm. Because it known that, any type of information requires more effort during encryption and decryption. Proposed algorithm will enhanced efficiency of encryption/decryption algorithm as compare to existing algorithms. Finally, expected results are showing the performance of the proposed algorithm

1) Confidentiality

Confidentiality is the concept of ensuring that data is not made available or disclosed to unauthorized people.

Confidentially is achieved through encryption. Both symmetric and asymmetric encryption can be used and we'll discuss them later.
Confidentiality was the original purpose of cryptography. If the data is confidential, it cannot be read or understood by anyone other than the intended recipient or recipients.
The "secret spy ring" you might have gotten in a box of cereal when you were a kid is an example. Typically, with the aid of the ring,

you substitute each   letter in your message with another letter. Unless someone looking at the now   encrypted   data   knows   the encryption key, i.e. has an equivalent ring or   understands   how   it works, they cannot read the original message - at least not   trivially.

Confidentiality of data is accomplished by using strong encryption algorithms   that cannot be easily "broken." A secret spy ring doing simple character   substitution is not strong encryption,   but probably strong enough for two kids   playing spy.

Confidentiality is important when network communications are of a sensitive   nature, such as trade secrets, client information subject to privacy laws or   policies, or business strategies that depend on the element of surprise.

Confidentiality is also important for important data at rest, i.e. not transferring the network.

2) Data Integrity

Data integrity is the protection of information from damage or deliberate   manipulation. In plain language, integrity insures that data hasn't been   modified. Integrity is obviously extremely critical for any kind of business or   electronic commerce. Imagine if someone could modify invoices or financial   records without detection.

Hash algorithms are typically used to provide for integrity of information.

We'll discuss hashing later, but consider a hash to be like a fingerprint of the   data whose integrity you want to protect. If the data is modified, even a single   bit changed, the fingerprint or hash is different, and the modification detected.

The hash itself is usually encrypted. If someone could modify the data and   then modify the hash to match it, the modification might go unnoticed.   Encrypting the hash value prevents this.

Integrity is less resource intensive than confidentiality - full data encryption. Also, some countries legally restrict encrypted data from flowing across their   borders, for example France and Israel. Of course plenty of encrypted Internet   traffic does anyway, but it can be a legal concern.

3) Authentication

Authentication is the concept of uniquely identifying individuals to provide   assurance of a user's identity. In others words, proving people are who you   claim they. Are Typical physical and logical authentication methods include the use of ID cards, door locks and keys, and network logins and passwords.

For example, when I arrived at the airport yesterday, I identified myself to the airline gate agent as I fumbled through my pockets for my password.

"Hi, I'm Ted Demopoulos." This is just identification, just a claim. I authenticated myself, proved that in fact I am Ted Demopoulos, by providing my passport. Traditionally we have authenticated identities based on one of three attributes:

Something the person knows, such as a password

Something the person has, such as a token

Something the person is, or biometrics

In addition, we can authenticate based on a fourth attribute:

Encryption is used by all three authentication methods. No matter what you use to authenticate, you want to make sure the information is protected as it travels the network and that it is also secure when it resides on the backend server

4.6 Model Development

The development of a model is a key step in solving a problem. Once model is generated then we can develop an algorithm, we can translate it into a computer program in some programming language. Our model development process consists of five major steps.

Step 1: Obtain a description of the problem.

Step 2: Analyze the problem.

Step 3: Develop a model.

Step 4: Refine the model by adding more detail.

Step 5: Review the model.

Step 1: Obtain a description of the problem.

This step is much more difficult than it appears. In the following discussion, the word *client* refers to someone who wants to find a solution to a problem, and the word *developer* refers to someone who finds a way to solve the problem. The developer must create an algorithm that will solve the client's problem.

The client is responsible for creating a description of the problem, but this is often the weakest part of the process. It's quite common for a problem description to suffer from one or more of the following types of defects: (1) the description relies on implicit assumptions, (2) the description is uncertain, (3) the description is incomplete, or (4) the description has internal contradictions. These defects are seldom due to carelessness by the client. Instead, they are due to the fact that natural languages (English, French, Korean, etc.) are rather imprecise. Part of the developer's responsibility is to identify defects in the description of a problem, and to work with the client to remedy those defects

Step 2: Analyze the problem.

The purpose of this step is to determine both the starting and ending points for solving the problem. This process is analogous to a mathematician determining what is given and what must be proven. A good problem description makes it easier to perform this step.

When determining the starting point, we should start by seeking answers to the following questions:

- What data are available?
- Where is that data?
- What formulas pertain to the problem?
- What rules exist for working with the data?
- What relationships exist among the data values?

When determining the ending point, we need to describe the characteristics of a solution. In other words, how will we know when we're done? Asking the following questions often helps to determine the ending point.

- What new facts will we have?
- What items will have changed?
- What changes will have been made to those items?
- What things will no longer exist?

Step 3: Develop a model.

An algorithm is a plan for solving a problem, but plans come in several levels of detail. It's usually better to start with a high-level algorithm that includes the major part of a solution, but leaves the details until later. We can use an everyday example to demonstrate a high-level algorithm.

Problem: I need a send a birthday card to my brother, Mark.

Analysis: I don't have a card. I prefer to buy a card rather than make one myself.

High-level algorithm:
Go to a store that sells greeting cards
Get the Plain Text and Secrete Key
Convert it into Cipher Text
sent to the Other Person
This Person Get Cipher text and Decrypt it

This algorithm is satisfactory for daily use, but it lacks details that would have to be added were a computer to carry out the solution. These details include answers to questions such as the following.

- Which Data and key will I take?
- How will I get that: Ascii, Binary, Hexadecimal, Octal?
- Which kind of description technique are used

These kinds of details are considered in the next step of our process.

Step 4: Refine the model by adding more detail.

An algorithm shows the major steps that need to be followed to solve a problem. Now we need to add details to these steps, but how much detail should we add? Unfortunately, the answer to this question depends on the situation. We have to consider who (or what) is going to implement the algorithm and how much that person (or thing) already knows how to do. If someone is going to sent Secrete text, then not that person is familiar with Encryption process in the community and how well the Decrypt key in another person

When our goal is to develop algorithms that will lead to computer programs, we need to consider the capabilities of the computer and provide enough detail so that someone else could use our algorithm to write a computer program that follows the steps in our algorithm. As with the Decryption problem, we need to adjust the level of detail to match the ability of the programmer. When in doubt, or when you are learning, it is better to have too much detail than to have too little.

Most of our examples will move from a high-level to a detailed algorithm in a single step, but this is not always reasonable. For larger, more complex problems, it is common to go through this process several times, developing intermediate level algorithms as we go. Each time, we add more detail to the previous algorithm, stopping when we see no benefit to further refinement. This technique of gradually working from a high-level to a detailed algorithm is often called stepwise refinement.

Step 5: Review the model.

The final step is to review the model. What are we looking for? First, we need to work through the algorithm step by step to determine whether or not it will solve the original problem. Once we are satisfied that the algorithm does provide a solution to the problem, we start to look for other things. The following questions are typical of ones that should be asked whenever we review an algorithm. Asking these questions and seeking their answers is a good way to develop skills that can be applied to the next problem.

4.7 Development of proposed Algorithm
4.7.1 Model generation

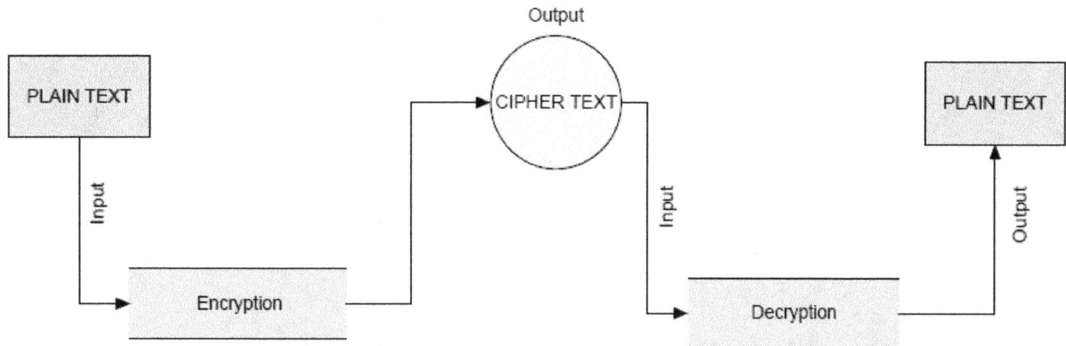

Fig-4.1

4.7.2 ER Diagram of model

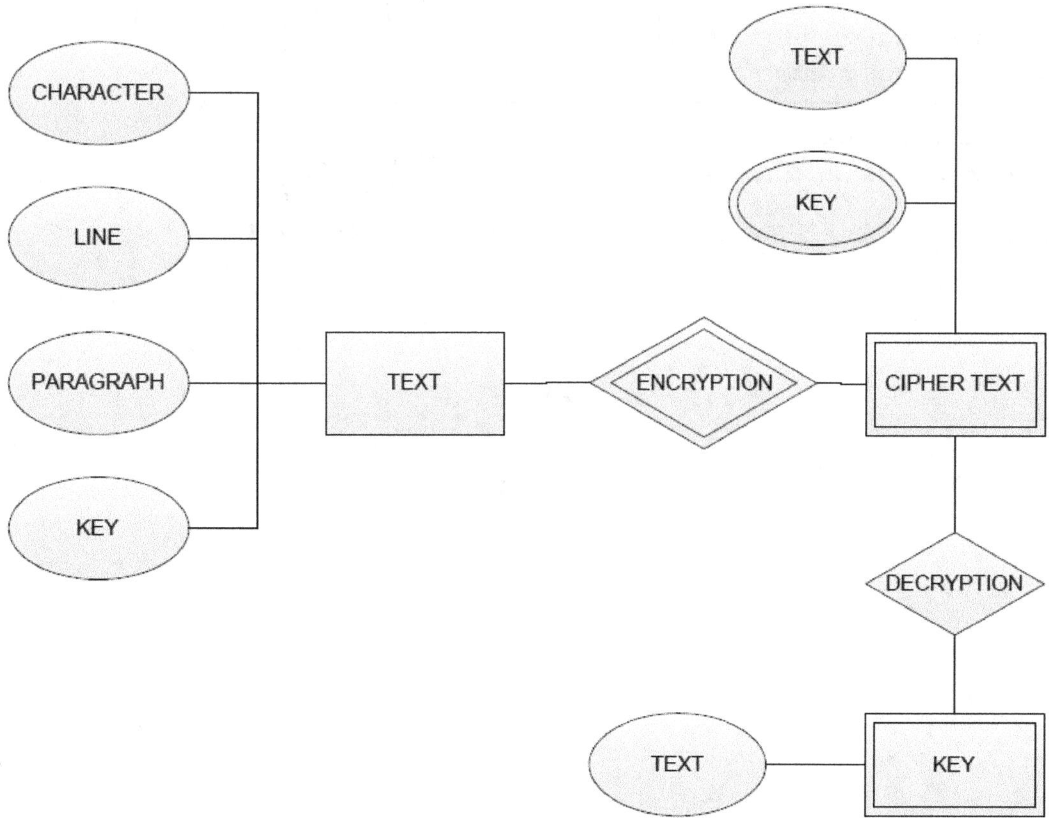

Fig-4.2

4.7.3 Flow Chart of Model

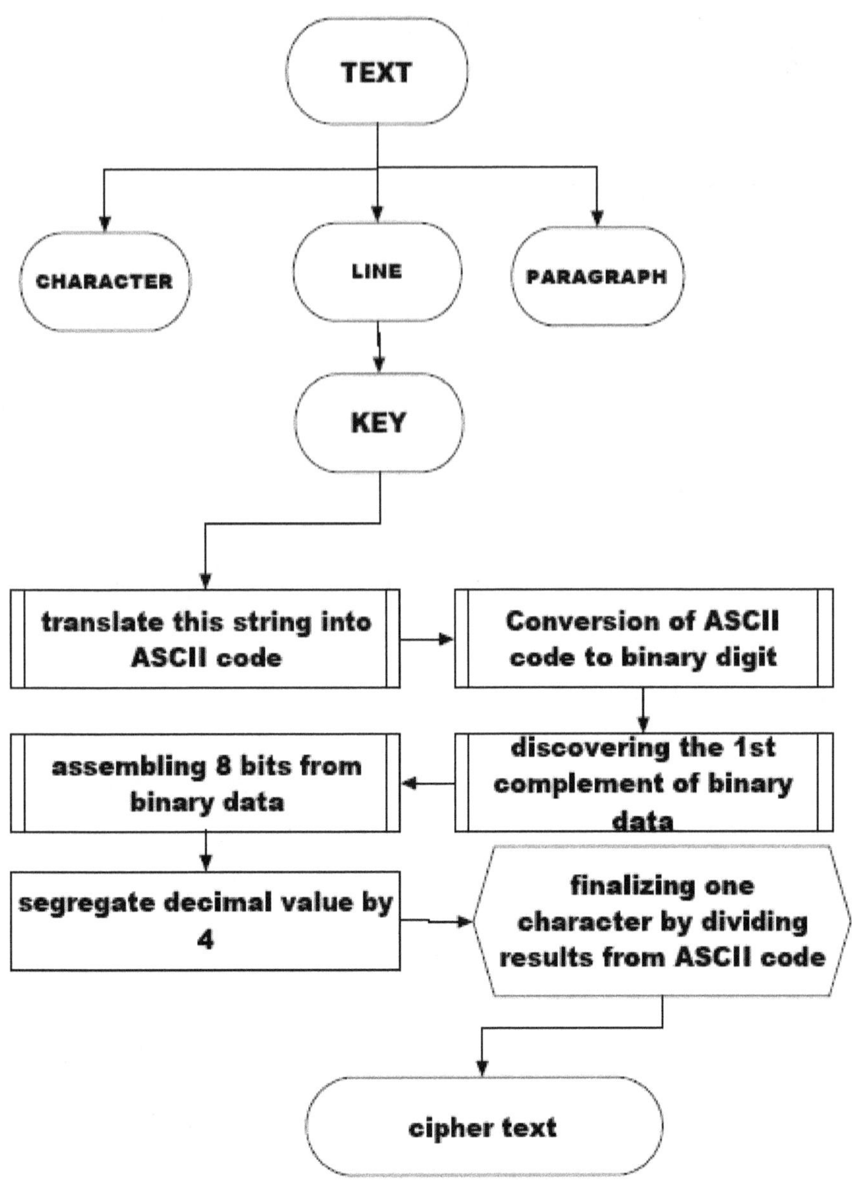

Fig: 4.3

4.8 New Model Process Steps
4.8.1 Encryption algorithm

Step-1 – Input source data and key

The simple text (character, line or paragraph) is taken as input from the user and a variable length key is also taken as input from the user for the purpose of encryption.

Reason for taking a key:

The Cipher text can be available in public however a unique key is only made available to the authenticated user and without it decryption cannot be carried out.

Step-2 - adding the key with the source data

In this step we combine text and key, Reason for joining simple text with key

The key is a unique sequence of characters made available only to the authenticated user and therefore combination of key and source data will increase the complexity of the original data. In algorithms RSA, DSA and ELGAMAL this feature is not included.

Step-3 – Convert each character of this string into ASCII code

Reason for using ASCII code, ASCII code is used in encryption and decryption algorithm because ASCII code can store character from more than one language and with more than 250 characters per language. Size of ASCII code is very small i.e. 1 byte per character, it is platform independent and in some cases it can speed up access to individual characters.

Step-4 - Conversion of ASCII code to binary digit

If the converted binary number is less than 8 bits it is preceded by 0S.

Reason for using binary code:

Binary devices are platform independent, simple and easy to build and also binary signals are Unambiguous (which gives them noise immunity). Flawless copies can be made of binary data. Anything that can be represented with some sort of pattern can be represented with patterns of bits.

Step-5 - Calculate the 1st complement of binary data

Swap the 0s and 1s in the resultant binary number that is obtained in the previous step. So a complement of the whole binary number is   obtained.

Reason for using 1s complement:

By taking 1s complement of the binary data obtained in previous step, we can avoid any direct conversion of binary data into simple text therefore making encryption stronger.

2s complement takes slightly longer to form the negative of a number, whereas 1s complement is quicker, 2s complement has an asymmetrical range, so the largest negative number causes overflow if you try to make it positive, which does not happen with 1s complement.

Step-6 - Assembling 8 bits from binary data and obtain decimal value.

Now each binary octet is converted into decimal value.

Reason for converting binary data into decimal data:

Even though 1s complement of the actual binary data is taken, the final cipher text has to appear in the format of plain text and not binary code. Therefore the binary code is converted into decimal code by taking octets (8 bits) and converting each octet into a decimal value.

Step – 7 - Divide decimal value by 4 and obtain ASCII value of result & remainder.

Each decimal value obtained in the previous step is divided by 4. ASCII value of the result obtained is noted. The remainder of that calculation is noted. The remainder value is put on right side to the ASCII value.

Reason for segregation:

The decimal value obtained previously is divided by 4 which is an arbitrary number and any number can be chosen instead of 4. The rest of the operation mentioned above is only for the purpose of strengthening the encryption process. Finally the combination of all the previously obtained values is treated as Cipher text.

4.8.2 Decryption algorithm

Step-1 - Receiving cipher text and key

This is the initial step for decryption. In decryption cipher text is used along with a secret key to perform the next step.

Step-2 Convert the entire cipher text into ASCII code.

Starting from first character combine each alternate character to obtain ASCII code.

Step-3 Multiplication of ASCII code of the first character by 4 and get Decimal value

Find decimal value of each ASCII code and multiply with 4.

Step-4 – Convert decimal into binary data

Step-5 - Calculating one's complement of binary data

For calculating one's complement the previously obtained binary data is reversed that is 0s and 1s are swapped.

Step-6 Obtain Decimal value by gathering each 8 bits from previous data

Divide data in group of 8 bits and find decimal value

Step-7 Translating the previous ASCII code into source data and remove key

Convert all decimal value into ASCII code.

4.9 COMPARISION, PERFORMANCE MEASUREMENT AND CORRELATION BETWEEN SUGGESTED ALGORITHM AND OTHER ALGORITHMS (TEXT DATA)

Windows XP BITLENGTH 512				
CHARACTER				
	1	2	3	4
SAMPLE	RSA	DSA	ELGAMAL	PKA
1	2	2	3	2
2	4	2	2	4
3	2	2	1	2
4	1	2	1	1
5	1	2	2	2
MEAN	**2**	**2**	**1.8**	**2.2**
VARIANCE	**1.5**	**0**	**0.7**	**1.2**

Table 4.1

Here, variance of PKA is moderate compared to others, but variance of DSA is zero. Performance of PKA is moderate.

Windows XP BITLENGTH 1024				
CHARACTER				
	1	2	3	4
SAMPLE	RSA	DSA	ELGAMAL	PKA
1	3	2	2	2
2	5	2	4	2
3	3	2	3	1
4	2	3	2	2
5	4	2	2	3
MEAN	**3.4**	**2.2**	**2.6**	**2**
VARIANCE	**1.3**	**0.2**	**0.8**	**0.5**

Table 4.2

Here, variance of PKA is moderate compared to others, but variance of DSA is 0.2 Performance of PKA is moderate.

<table>
<tr><td colspan="6" align="center">Windows XP BITLENGTH 2048</td></tr>
<tr><td colspan="6" align="center">CHARACTER</td></tr>
<tr><td></td><td>1</td><td>2</td><td>3</td><td>4</td></tr>
<tr><td>SAMPLE</td><td>RSA</td><td>DSA</td><td>ELGAMAL</td><td>PKA</td></tr>
<tr><td>1</td><td>57</td><td>2</td><td>22</td><td>1</td></tr>
<tr><td>2</td><td>11</td><td>1</td><td>19</td><td>1</td></tr>
<tr><td>3</td><td>75</td><td>2</td><td>35</td><td>2</td></tr>
<tr><td>4</td><td>28</td><td>1</td><td>52</td><td>2</td></tr>
<tr><td>5</td><td>17</td><td>2</td><td>14</td><td>1</td></tr>
<tr><td>MEAN</td><td>37.6</td><td>1.6</td><td>28.4</td><td>1.4</td></tr>
<tr><td>VARIANCE</td><td>749.8</td><td>0.3</td><td>234.3</td><td>0.3</td></tr>
</table>

Table 4.3

Here, variance of PKA and DSA is lowest, performance of PKA and DSA is best.

<table>
<tr><td colspan="5" align="center">Windows XP BITLENGTH 512</td></tr>
<tr><td colspan="5" align="center">LINE</td></tr>
<tr><td>SAMPLE</td><td>RSA</td><td>DSA</td><td>ELGAMAL</td><td>PKA</td></tr>
<tr><td>1</td><td>2</td><td>2</td><td>1</td><td>3</td></tr>
<tr><td>2</td><td>1</td><td>2</td><td>2</td><td>2</td></tr>
<tr><td>3</td><td>1</td><td>2</td><td>2</td><td>2</td></tr>
<tr><td>4</td><td>1</td><td>2</td><td>2</td><td>3</td></tr>
<tr><td>5</td><td>1</td><td>3</td><td>2</td><td>2</td></tr>
<tr><td>MEAN</td><td>1.2</td><td>2.2</td><td>1.8</td><td>2.4</td></tr>
<tr><td>VARIANCE</td><td>0.2</td><td>0.2</td><td>0.2</td><td>0.3</td></tr>
</table>

Table 4.4

Here, variance of PKA is highest; performance of PKA is weak compared to others.

<table>
<tr><td colspan="5" align="center">Windows XP BITLENGTH 1024</td></tr>
<tr><td colspan="5" align="center">LINE</td></tr>
<tr><td>SAMPLE</td><td>RSA</td><td>DSA</td><td>ELGAMAL</td><td>PKA</td></tr>
<tr><td>1</td><td>3</td><td>2</td><td>5</td><td>2</td></tr>
<tr><td>2</td><td>5</td><td>3</td><td>5</td><td>1</td></tr>
<tr><td>3</td><td>6</td><td>2</td><td>4</td><td>3</td></tr>
<tr><td>4</td><td>4</td><td>2</td><td>2</td><td>2</td></tr>
<tr><td>5</td><td>2</td><td>2</td><td>5</td><td>2</td></tr>
<tr><td>MEAN</td><td>4</td><td>2.2</td><td>4.2</td><td>2</td></tr>
<tr><td>VARIANCE</td><td>2.5</td><td>0.2</td><td>1.7</td><td>0.5</td></tr>
</table>

Table 4.5

Here, variance of PKA is moderate compared to others, but variance of DSA is 0.2 Performance of PKA is moderate.

Windows XP BITLENGTH 2048				
LINE				
SAMPLE	RSA	DSA	ELGAMAL	PKA
1	14	2	12	2
2	28	3	42	1
3	30	2	30	3
4	10	2	20	2
5	49	3	23	3
MEAN	**26.2**	**2.4**	**25.4**	**2.2**
VARIANCE	**237.2**	**0.3**	**127.8**	**0.7**

Table 4.6

Here, variance of PKA is moderate compared to others, but variance of DSA is 0.3. Performance of PKA is moderate.

Windows XP BITLENGTH 512				
PARAGRAPH				
SAMPLE	RSA	DSA	ELGAMAL	PKA
1	2	3	1	2
2	1	3	3	2
3	1	3	2	3
4	1	2	2	2
5	1	2	2	2
MEAN	**1.2**	**2.6**	**2**	**2.2**
VARIANCE	**0.2**	**0.3**	**0.5**	**0.2**

Table 4.7

Here, variance of PKA and RSA is lowest, performance of PKA and RSA is best.

Windows XP BITLENGTH 1024				
PARAGRAPH				
SAMPLE	RSA	DSA	ELGAMAL	PKA
1	4	2	4	3
2	4	3	4	2
3	3	3	5	3
4	3	3	5	2
5	3	3	6	2
MEAN	**3.4**	**2.8**	**4.8**	**2.4**
VARIANCE	**0.3**	**0.2**	**0.7**	**0.3**

Table 4.8

Here, variance of PKA is moderate compared to others, but variance of DSA is 0.2. Performance of PKA is moderate.

Windows XP BITLENGTH 2048				
PARAGRAPH				
SAMPLE	RSA	DSA	ELGAMAL	PKA
1	8	3	28	2
2	73	2	22	2
3	23	3	28	1
4	27	3	39	2
5	11	2	37	3
MEAN	**28.4**	**2.6**	**30.8**	**2**
VARIANCE	**684.8**	**0.3**	**49.7**	**0.5**

Table 4.9

Here, variance of PKA is moderate compared to others, but variance of DSA is 0.3. Performance of PKA is moderate.

Windows 7 BITLENGTH 512				
CHARACTER MEAURE IN SECOND				
	1	2	3	4
SAMPLE	RSA	DSA	ELGAMAL	PKA
1	3	2	4	3
2	2	2	2	2
3	2	3	2	2
4	2	2	2	1
5	2	3	2	2
MEAN	**2.2**	**2.4**	**2.4**	**2**
VARIANCE	**0.2**	**0.3**	**0.8**	**0.5**

Table 4.10

Here, variance of PKA is moderate compared to others, but variance of RSA is 0.2. Performance of PKA is moderate.

Windows 7 BITLENGTH 1024				
CHARACTER MEAURE IN SECOND				
	1	2	3	4
SAMPLE	RSA	DSA	ELGAMAL	PKA
1	7	2	6	3
2	4	3	4	3
3	3	3	3	2
4	3	2	7	2
5	5	2	7	1
MEAN	**4.4**	**2.4**	**5.4**	**2.2**
VARIANCE	**2.8**	**0.3**	**3.3**	**0.7**

Table 4.11

Here, variance of PKA is moderate compared to others, but variance of DSA is 0.3. Performance of PKA is moderate.

Windows 7 BITLENGTH 2048				
CHARACTER MEAURE IN SECOND				
	1	2	3	4
SAMPLE	RSA	DSA	ELGAMAL	PKA
1	35	2	57	3
2	28	2	83	2
3	44	3	27	2
4	23	3	13	2
5	12	2	100	2
MEAN	**28.4**	**2.4**	**56**	**2.2**
VARIANCE	**146.3**	**0.3**	**1339**	**0.2**

Table 4.12

Here, variance of PKA is lowest, performance of PKA is best.

Windows 7 BITLENGTH 512				
LINE MEAURE IN SECOND				
SAMPLE	RSA	DSA	ELGAMAL	PKA
1	2	2	2	3
2	2	3	3	2
3	2	3	2	2
4	2	2	3	2
5	2	2	2	2
MEAN	**2**	**2.4**	**2.4**	**2.2**
VARIANCE	**0**	**0.3**	**0.3**	**0.2**

Table 4.13

Here, variance of PKA is moderate compared to others, but variance of RSA is zero. Performance of PKA is moderate.

Windows 7 BITLENGTH 1024				
LINE MEAURE IN SECOND				
SAMPLE	RSA	DSA	ELGAMAL	PKA
1	4	2	8	3
2	4	3	5	2
3	5	2	3	2
4	4	2	5	2
5	6	2	4	2
MEAN	**4.6**	**2.2**	**5**	**2.2**
VARIANCE	**0.8**	**0.2**	**3.5**	**0.2**

Table 4.14

Here, variance of PKA and DSA is lowest, performance of PKA and RSA is best.

Windows 7 BITLENGTH 2048				
LINE MEAURE IN SECOND				
SAMPLE	RSA	DSA	ELGAMAL	PKA
1	29	3	29	3
2	17	3	33	2
3	21	2	32	2
4	45	2	18	2
5	24	3	20	2
MEAN	**27.2**	**2.6**	**26.4**	**2.2**
VARIANCE	**118.2**	**0.3**	**48.3**	**0.2**

Table 4.15

Here, variance of PKA is lowest, performance of PKA is best.

Windows 7 BITLENGTH 512				
PARAGRAPH MEAURE IN SECOND				
SAMPLE	RSA	DSA	ELGAMAL	PKA
1	2	2	2	4
2	3	2	3	2
3	3	3	2	2
4	2	2	3	1
5	2	2	2	1
MEAN	**2.4**	**2.2**	**2.4**	**2**
VARIANCE	**0.3**	**0.2**	**0.3**	**1.5**

Table 4.16

Here, variance of PKA is weak compared to others, but variance of DSA is 0.2. Performance of PKA is weak

Windows 7 BITLENGTH 1024				
PARAGRAPH MEAURE IN SECOND				
SAMPLE	RSA	DSA	ELGAMAL	PKA
1	6	2	5	2
2	3	3	7	2
3	3	2	6	2
4	4	3	4	2
5	7	3	4	1
MEAN	**4.6**	**2.6**	**5.2**	**1.8**
VARIANCE	**3.3**	**0.3**	**1.7**	**0.2**

Table 4.17

Here, variance of PKA is lowest, performance of PKA is best.

Windows 7 BITLENGTH 2048
PARAGRAPH MEAURE IN SECOND

SAMPLE	RSA	DSA	ELGAMAL	PKA
1	36	2	34	2
2	16	3	27	2
3	10	2	29	2
4	10	2	27	2
5	46	3	45	1
MEAN	**23.6**	**2.4**	**32.4**	**1.8**
VARIANCE	**270.8**	**0.3**	**57.8**	**0.2**

Table 4.18

Here, variance of PKA is lowest, performance of PKA is best.

Windows 8 BITLENGTH 512				
CHARACTER				
	1	2	3	4
SAMPLE	RSA	DSA	ELGAMAL	PKA
1	2	3	3	3
2	2	2	2	2
3	3	2	2	2
4	3	2	1	2
5	2	1	1	1
MEAN	**2.4**	**2**	**1.8**	**2**
VARIANCE	**0.3**	**0.5**	**0.7**	**0.5**

Table 4.19

Here, variance of PKA is moderate compared to others, but variance of RSA is 0.3 Performance of PKA is moderate

Windows 8 BITLENGTH 1024				
CHARACTER				
	1	2	3	4
SAMPLE	RSA	DSA	ELGAMAL	PKA
1	5	3	7	2
2	2	2	2	2
3	2	3	3	2
4	3	2	4	2
5	4	2	3	3
MEAN	**3.2**	**2.4**	**3.8**	**2.2**
VARIANCE	**1.7**	**0.3**	**3.7**	**0.2**

Table 4.20

Here, variance of PKA is lowest, performance of PKA is best

Windows 8 BITLENGTH 2048				
CHARACTER				
	1	2	3	4
SAMPLE	RSA	DSA	ELGAMAL	PKA
1	35	3	13	3
2	22	3	30	3
3	33	2	6	3
4	20	2	30	2
5	28	3	20	2
MEAN	**27.6**	**2.6**	**19.8**	**2.6**
VARIANCE	**43.3**	**0.3**	**111.2**	**0.3**

Table 4.21

Here, variance of PKA and DSA is lowest, performance of PKA and DSA is best

Windows 8 BITLENGTH 512				
LINE				
SAMPLE	RSA	DSA	ELGAMAL	PKA
1	2	1	2	2
2	2	3	2	2
3	1	2	3	3
4	1	2	3	2
5	2	3	3	2
MEAN	**1.6**	**2.2**	**2.6**	**2.2**
VARIANCE	**0.3**	**0.7**	**0.3**	**0.2**

Table 4.22

Here, variance of PKA is lowest, performance of PKA is best

Windows 8 BITLENGTH 1024				
LINE				
SAMPLE	RSA	DSA	ELGAMAL	PKA
1	3	3	5	2
2	3	1	3	2
3	4	3	2	2
4	2	2	4	3
5	2	3	2	2
MEAN	**2.8**	**2.4**	**3.2**	**2.2**
VARIANCE	**0.7**	**0.8**	**1.7**	**0.2**

Table 4.23

Here, variance of PKA is lowest, performance of PKA is best

Windows 8 BITLENGTH 2048				
LINE				
SAMPLE	RSA	DSA	ELGAMAL	PKA
1	40	3	18	3
2	13	2	13	2
3	38	3	19	2
4	30	2	38	3
5	32	3	23	2
MEAN	**30.6**	**2.6**	**22.2**	**2.4**
VARIANCE	**113.8**	**0.3**	**90.7**	**0.3**

Table 4.24

Here, variance of PKA and DSA is lowest, performance of PKA and DSA is best

Windows 8 BITLENGTH 512				
PARAGRAPH				
SAMPLE	RSA	DSA	ELGAMAL	PKA
1	1	3	2	3
2	2	3	3	3
3	2	2	2	2
4	2	2	2	1
5	3	1	2	1
MEAN	**2**	**2.2**	**2.2**	**2**
VARIANCE	**0.5**	**0.7**	**0.2**	**1**

Table 4.25

Here, variance of PKA is weak compared to others, but variance of ELGAMAL is 0.2 Performance of PKA is weak.

Windows 8 BITLENGTH 1024				
PARAGRAPH				
SAMPLE	RSA	DSA	ELGAMAL	PKA
1	3	3	6	3
2	2	3	3	2
3	3	2	4	2
4	2	2	3	3
5	5	3	4	2
MEAN	**3**	**2.6**	**4**	**2.4**
VARIANCE	**1.5**	**0.3**	**1.5**	**0.3**

Table 4.26

Here, variance of PKA and DSA is lowest, performance of PKA and DSA is best

Windows 8 BITLENGTH 2048				
PARAGRAPH				
SAMPLE	RSA	DSA	ELGAMAL	PKA
1	46	3	24	3
2	39	3	20	2
3	40	3	40	3
4	38	2	39	3
5	38	2	28	2
MEAN	**40.2**	**2.6**	**30.2**	**2.6**
VARIANCE	**11.2**	**0.3**	**80.2**	**0.3**

Table 4.27

Here, variance of PKA and DSA is lowest, performance of PKA and DSA is best

4.10 COMPARISION, PERFORMANCE MEASUREMENT AND CORRELATION BETWEEN SUGGESTED ALGORITHM AND OTHER ALGORITHMS (AUDIO DATA)

We have measured correlation co-efficient of PKA for various audio files having different tone frequency. We considered some audio files for duration 0.30 second and 5 seconds.

Duration is 0 To 30 Second			
Tone Frequency	**Original size in MB**	**Encrypted size in MB**	**Time in second**
100	2.5	17.6	2
250	2.5	17.7	1
440	2.5	17.7	2
1000	2.5	17.7	1
10000	2.5	17.7	2
Correlation Co-efficient between Tone Frequency and Time in Second			0.37

Table 4.28

Duration is 0 To 5 Second			
Tone Frequency	ORIGINAL SIZE in MB	ENCRYPTED SIZE in MB	Time in second
100	0.4	2.96	1
250	0.4	2.96	1
440	0.4	2.96	2
1000	0.4	2.96	1
10000	0.4	2.96	2
Correlation Co-efficient between Tone Frequency and Time in Second			0.61

Table 4.29

We found interesting results when duration of audio file is 30 seconds then correlation. Co-efficient between Tone Frequency and Encryption time in second is 0.37 while duration is 5 seconds then correlation Co-efficient between Tone Frequency and Encryption time in second is 0.61. It shows that with decrees of time duration of audio file, the correlation co-efficient between Tone Frequency and Encryption time in second goes high. It can be concluded that PKA is affected by tone frequency in audio file.

4.11 COMPARISION, PERFORMANCE MEASUREMENT AND CORRELATION BETWEEN SUGGESTED ALGORITHM AND OTHER ALGORITHMS(IMAGE DATA)

We have considered various .BMP and .PNG type Image files and recorded original image file size and Encrypted image file size.

Cover Image	ORIGINAL SIZE (KB)	ENCRYPTED SIZE (KB)	Time in second
LOTUS.BMP	35	46.4	1
PEPPERS.BMP	33.4	44.2	1
SAINT.BMP	33.5	44.4	1
TIGER.BMP	34.4	45.9	1
Correlation Co-efficient between Original size and Encrypted Size			0.99

Table 4.30

<table>
<tr><td rowspan="2">Cover Image</td><td>ORIGINAL SIZE (KB)</td><td>ENCRYPTED SIZE (KB)</td><td>Time in second</td></tr>
<tr></tr>
<tr><td>BABOON.PNG</td><td>43.7</td><td>82.9</td><td>2</td></tr>
<tr><td>BONSAI.PNG</td><td>36.1</td><td>71.3</td><td>1</td></tr>
<tr><td>DOEL.PNG</td><td>36.2</td><td>57.8</td><td>1</td></tr>
<tr><td>LEENA.PNG</td><td>37.7</td><td>51.2</td><td>1</td></tr>
<tr><td colspan="3">Correlation Co-efficient between Original size and Encrypted Size</td><td>0.70</td></tr>
</table>

Table 4.31

Result shows that for BMP image file correlation co-efficient between original size and encrypted size is 0.99, it means if any change in original size, some change reflates in encrypted file while in PNG files, correlation co-efficient between original size and encrypted size is 0.70. It can be concluded that change is original size and encrypted size is less compared to BMP file.

4.12 VARIANCE ANALYSIS FOR ALL ALGORITHMS

We have compare and measured performance of RSA, DSA and ELGAMAL algorithms with PKA. We have considered various bit length, character length and various operating systems.

OS	TYPE	BITLENGTH	RSA	DSA	ELGAMAL	PKA
WINDOS XP	CHARACTER	2048	749.80	0.30	234.30	0.3
		1024	1.30	0.20	0.80	0.5
		512	1.50	0.00	0.70	1.2
	LINE	2048	237.20	0.30	127.80	0.7
		1024	2.50	0.20	1.70	0.5
		512	0.20	0.20	0.20	0.3
	PARAGRAPH	2048	684.80	0.30	49.70	0.5
		1024	0.30	0.20	0.70	0.3
		512	0.20	0.30	0.50	0.2
WINDOWS 7	CHARACTER	2048	146.30	0.30	1339.00	0.2
		1024	2.80	0.30	3.30	0.7
		512	0.20	0.30	0.80	0.5
	LINE	2048	118.20	0.30	48.30	0.2
		1024	0.80	0.20	3.50	0.2
		512	0.00	0.30	0.30	0.2

		2048	270.80	0.30	57.80	0.2
	PARAGRAPH	1024	3.30	0.30	1.70	0.2
		512	0.30	0.20	0.30	1.5
		2048	43.30	0.30	111.20	0.3
	CHARACTER	1024	1.70	0.30	3.70	0.2
		512	0.30	0.50	0.70	0.5
		2048	113.80	0.30	90.70	0.3
WIDOWS 8	LINE	1024	0.70	0.80	1.70	0.2
		512	0.30	0.70	0.30	0.2
		2048	11.20	0.30	80.20	0.3
	PARAGRAPH	1024	1.50	0.30	1.50	0.3
		512	0.50	0.70	0.20	1

The table shows PKA is best for 14 times, moderates for 10 times and weak for 3 times.

PKA's performance is weak for windows 7 and windows 8 operating systems for bit length 512 and in paragraph, windows XP bit length 512 and in Line.

PKA's performance is almost best among the RSA, DSA and ELGAMAL for windows 7 and windows 8 operating system.

4.13 Encryption & Decryption process of Text Data
4.13.1 PKA Working with Text Data

Plain text	P	N	A	K
Key	**369&**			
Add Key into text	**369&PnAk**			
Ascii code	**51545738801106575**			
Binary code	**00110011 00110110 00111001 00100110 01010000 01101110 01000001 01001011**			
1st complement	**11001100 11001001 11000110 11011001 10101111 10010001 10111110 10110100**			
Decimal value	**20420119821717 5145190180**			
Segregate BY 4	**30211261+3$1/2-0**			
Cipher text	**30211261+3$1/2-0**			

Table-4.33

Cipher text	**30211261+3$1/2-0**
Key	**369&**
Add Key into text	**369&30211261+3$1/2%0**

Ascii code	**3216+$/-**
Multiplication by 4	**20420019621617214418 8180**
Binary code	**1100110011001001110001101101100110101111100100011 011111010110100**
1st complement	**0011001100110110001110010010011001010000011011100 100000101001011**
Decimal value	**801106575**
Plain text	**PnAk**

Table. 4.34

4.13.2 PKA Working with Image Data

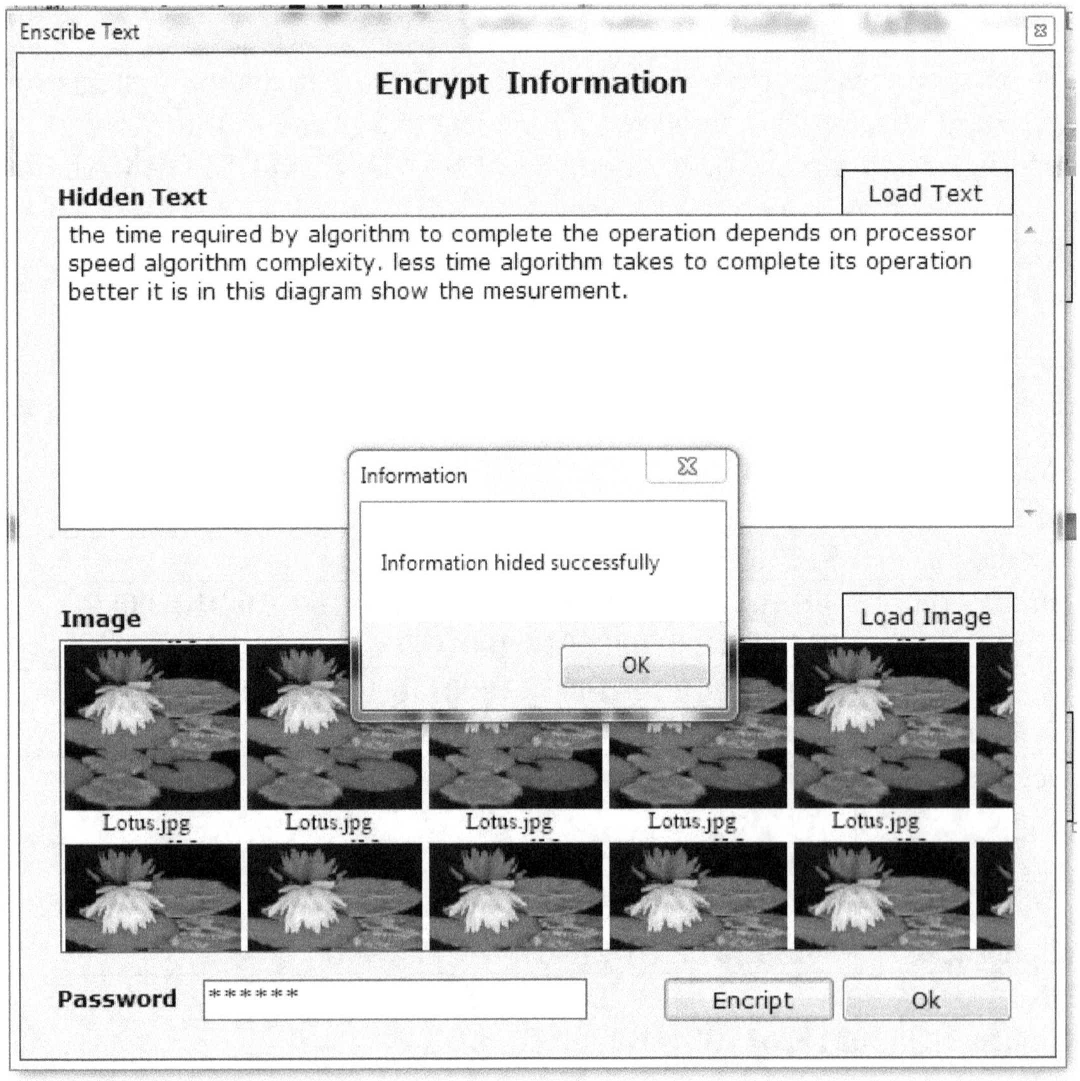

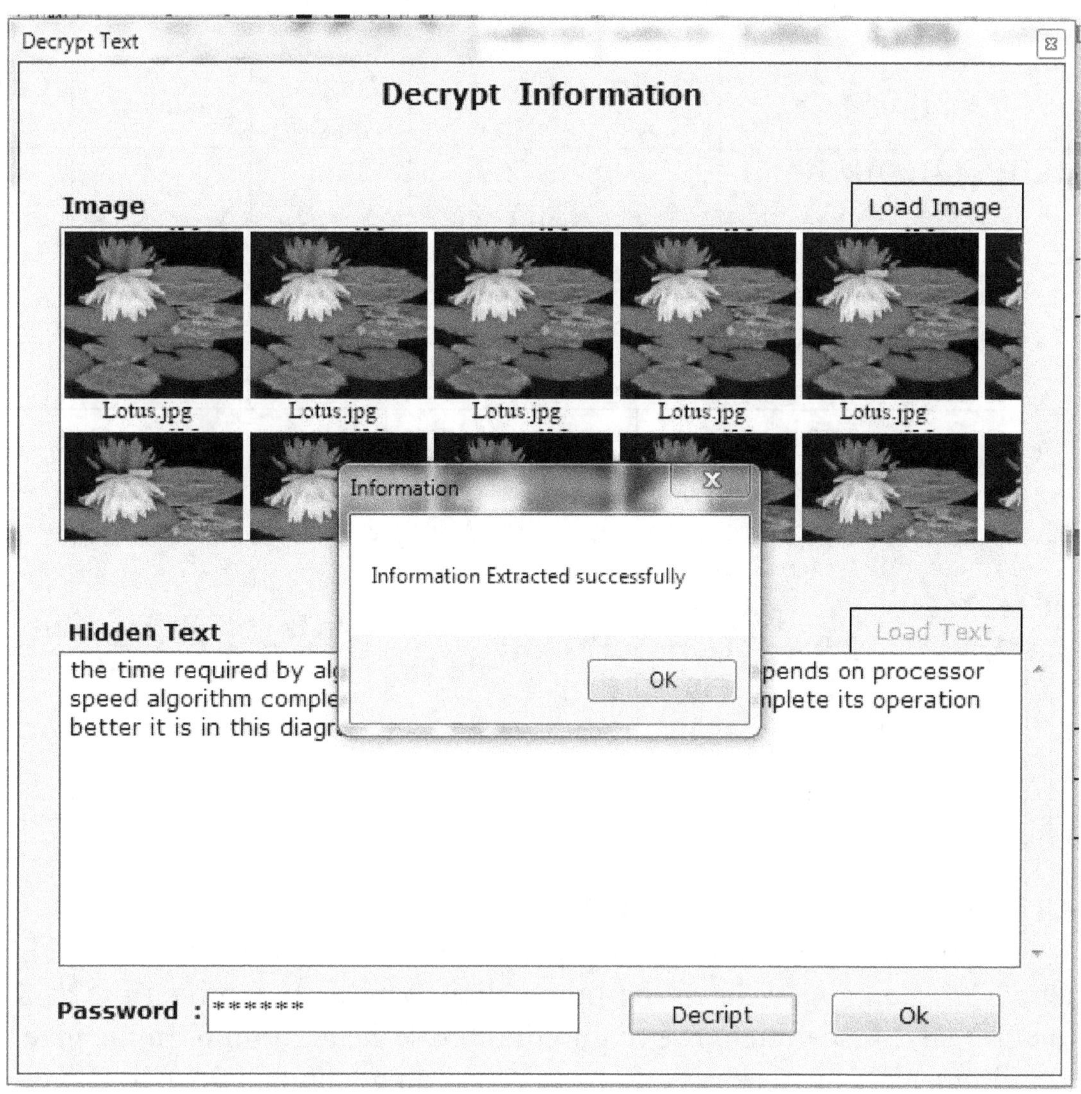

Decrypt Text
Decrypt Information
Image
Load Image
Lotus.jpg
Lotus.jpg
Lotus.jpg
Lotus.jpg
Lotus.jpg
Information
X
Information Extracted successfully
OK
Hidden Text
Load Text
the time required by al   pends on processor
speed algorithm comple   nplete its operation
better it is in this diagr
Password : ******
Decript
Ok

4.13.3 PKA Working with Audio Data

Audio File	Audio Size	Cipher Size	Original Message	Password	Cipher Text (PKA)
1kHz_44100Hz_16bit_05sec.WAV	430 KB	369 Character OR 3030 Bits	PnAK	123456	30211261+3$1/2-0

Cipher Text	Audio Size	Cipher Size	Password	Original Text	Audio File
30211261+3$1/2-0	2.96 MB	369 Character OR 3030 Bits	123456	PnAk	1kHz_44100Hz_16bit_05sec.WAV

4.13.4 Complexity of the algorithm by its strength

Complexities can also be expressed as orders of magnitude. If the length of the key is k, then the processing complexity is given by 2k. It means that 2 k operations are required to break the algorithm. In the given algorithm alphanumeric key is used. This alphanumeric key is Binary, ASCII. Division, multiplication, complements method. This provides the necessary strength to the algorithm. Thus known the algorithm, known the cipher text it is quite difficult to generate the alphanumeric key. Thus in the present algorithm, there is no means by which the key can be retrieved, other than trying all the combinations of key, the complexity of the algorithm is said to be exponential in nature.

Avalanche effect

In this model a sequence is generated and this sequence is substituted for the plain text to generate cipher text. Depending on the key, the sequence will be generated. We will identify the variations in the sequence generated, by slight variations in the key .Thus we can identify the variations in the cipher text by slight variations in the key considered. We will also identify the variations in the cipher text by slight variations in the plain text. For example, considering different cases for slight variations in the key

Case 1

Plain Text	P	n	A	K
Key Considered	&369			
Cipher Text	61302112+3$1/2%0			

Case 2

Plain Text	P	n	A	K
Key Considered	#123			
Cipher Text	70323130+3$1/2%0			

Case 3

Plain Text	P	n	A	K
Key Considered	!0%			
Cipher Text	723362+3$1/2%0			

Thus we can see that, by changing the key slightly, there are a lot of variations in the cipher text which provides maximum avalanche effect to the algorithm. This provides for maximum strength and security to the algorithm. But since the model is a simple substitution algorithm, the plain text variations to cipher text variations is negligible.

4.13.5 Security Analysis

The model uses a symptom purpose on the product of key to generate the sequence. The symptom purpose converts all values to BINARY, ASCII, and complement method .This sequence is substituted for plain text to generate cipher text. Thus it is impossible to generate the key from the known plain text and cipher texts. Thus this model is free from differential crypto analysis.

But this model uses a simple substitution technique to generate cipher text; it is somewhat susceptible to linear crypto analysis. The Key cannot be gained and not a whole of information can be gained, but part of information may be gained in this model. This algorithm is completely free from cipher text only, type of attack. By the other attacks, the key may not be retrieved but a part of plain text may be retrieved.

4.14 Multiple correlations Coefficient

In multiple correlations we study three or more variables at a time. Where as in case of partial correlation we study the relationship of two variable by making the other variables constant, in case of multiple correlation the effect of all the independent variables on dependent variables is studied.

The Sample Multiple Correlation Coefficient, R, is a measure of the strength of the association between the independent (explanatory) variables and the one dependent (prediction) variable.

Dependent variable is denoted by X1 and the independent variables by X2, X3, X4.... The coefficient of multiple linear correlation is denoted by R and the necessary subscript are added to it

For examples we have three variables X1, X2, X3 then

$R_{1.23}$ = Multiples correlation coefficient with X1 as dependent variable and X2 and X3 are independent variables.

$$R_{1.23} = \sqrt{(\square^2 12 + \square^2 13 - 2(\square 12 * \square 13 * \square 23))/1 - \square^2 23}$$

$R_{2.13}$ = Multiples correlation coefficient with X2 as dependent variable and X1 and X3 are independent variables.

$$R_{2.13} = \sqrt{(\square^2 21 + \square^2 23 - 2(\square 12 * \square 13 * \square 23))/1 - \square^2 13}$$

$R_{3.12}$ = Multiples correlation coefficient with X3 as dependent variable and X1 and X2 are independent variables. [8]

$$R_{3.12} = \sqrt{(\square^2 31 + \square^2 32 - 2(\square 12 * \square 13 * \square 23))/1 - \square^2 12}$$

Interpretation of Multiple correlation coefficient R

R value	Interpretation
1	Perfect Linear Relationship
0	No Linear Relationship
0.9	Strong Association
0.5	Moderate Association
0.25	Weak Association

Following is multiple correlation analysis table-39 of new algorithm PKA with three algorithms RSA DSA ELGAMAL. We want to observe the effect of PKA algorithm in other three algorithms or not.

Windows XP

   1) Character wise

      • **512 bit length**

     $R_{p.rd}$ = impossible

         Multiples Correlation coefficient between three algorithms (PKA is considered as dependent variable and RSA and DSA are considered as independent variable) is impossible, because linear correlation does not exist between some of two variables.

     $R_{p.re}$ = 0.79

The result of $R_{p.re}$ indicates near to strong relation between PKA and RSA, ELGAMAL. It suggests that PKA algorithm depends on RSA and ELGAMAL.

$R_{p.de}$ = impossible

Multiples Correlation coefficient between three algorithms (PKA is considered as dependent variable and DSA and ELGAMAL are considered as independent variable) is impossible, because linear correlation does not exist between some of two variables.

- **1024 bit length**

$R_{p.rd}$ = 0.92

The result of $R_{p.rd}$ indicates strong relation between PKA and RSA, DSA. It suggests that PKA algorithm strongly depends on RSA and DSA.

$R_{p.re}$ = 0.49

The result of $R_{p.re}$ indicates near to moderate relation between PKA and RSA, ELGAMAL. It suggests that PKA algorithm is not full depends on RSA and ELGAMAL.

$R_{p.de}$ = 0.92

The result of $R_{p.de}$ indicates strong relation between PKA and DSA, ELGAMAL. It suggests that PKA algorithm strongly depends on DSA and ELGAMAL.

- **2048 bit length**

$R_{p.rd}$ = 1.00

The result of $R_{p.rd}$ indicates Perfect Linear relation between PKA and RSA, DSA. It suggests that PKA algorithm is perfect depends on RSA and DSA.

$R_{p.re}$ = 0.85

The result of $R_{p.re}$ indicates near to strong relation between PKA and RSA, ELGAMAL. It suggests that PKA algorithm is some strong depends on RSA and ELGAMAL.

$R_{p.de}$ = 1.00

The result of $R_{p.de}$ indicates perfect linear relation between PKA and DSA, ELGAMAL. It suggests that PKA algorithm perfect depends on DSA and ELGAMAL.

2) **Line wise**

- **512 bit length**

$R_{p.rd}$ = 0.89

The result of $R_{p.rd}$ indicates near to strong relation between PKA and RSA, DSA. It suggests that PKA algorithm strongly depends on RSA and DSA.

$R_{p.re}$ = impossible

Multiples Correlation coefficient between three algorithms (PKA is considered as dependent variable and RSA and ELGAMAL are considered as independent variable) is impossible, because linear correlation does not exist between some of two variables.

$$R_{p.de} = 0.89$$

The result of $R_{p.de}$ indicates near to strong relation between PKA and DSA, ELGAMAL It suggests that PKA algorithm strongly depends on DSA and ELGAMAL.

- **1024 bit length**

$$R_{p.rd} = 0.62$$

The result of $R_{p.rd}$ indicates near to moderate relation between PKA and RSA, DSA. It suggests that PKA algorithm is some moderate depends on RSA and DSA.

$$R_{p.re} = 0.52$$

The result of $R_{p.re}$ indicates near moderate relation between PKA and RSA, ELGAMAL. It suggests that PKA algorithm moderately depends on RSA and ELGAMAL.

$$R_{p.de} = 0.96$$

The result of $R_{p.de}$ indicates near to strong relation between PKA and DSA, ELGAMAL It suggests that PKA algorithm depends on DSA and ELGAMAL.

- **2048 bit length**

$$R_{p.rd} = 0.99$$

The result of $R_{p.rd}$ indicates strong relation between PKA and RSA, DSA. It suggests that PKA algorithm strongly depends on RSA and DSA.

$$R_{p.re} = 0.81$$

The result of $R_{p.re}$ indicates near to strong relation between PKA and RSA, ELGAMAL. It suggests that PKA algorithm moderately depends on RSA and ELGAMAL.

$$R_{p.de} = 0.17$$

The result of $R_{p.de}$ indicates weak relation between PKA and DSA, ELGAMAL It suggests that PKA algorithm does not depend on DSA and ELGAMAL.

3) Paragraph wise

- **512 bit length**

$$R_{p.rd} = 0.61$$

The result of $R_{p.rd}$ indicates near to moderate relation between PKA and RSA, DSA. It suggests that PKA algorithm moderately depends on RSA and DSA.

$$R_{p.re} = 0.41$$

The result of $R_{p.re}$ indicates near to moderate relation between PKA and RSA, ELAGAMAL. It suggests that PKA algorithm moderately depends on RSA and ELAGAMAL.

$R_{p.de}$ = 0.41

The result of $R_{p.de}$ indicates near to Moderate relation between PKA and DSA, ELGAMAL It suggests that PKA algorithm moderately depends on DSA and ELGAMAL.

- **1024 bit length**

$R_{p.rd}$ = 0.67

The result of $R_{p.rd}$ indicates near to strong relation between PKA and RSA, DSA. It suggests that PKA algorithm strongly depends on RSA and DSA.

$R_{p.re}$ = 0.41

The result of $R_{p.re}$ indicates near to moderate relation between PKA and RSA, ELGAMAL. It suggests that PKA algorithm moderately depends on RSA and ELGAMAL.

$R_{p.de}$ = 0.61

The result of $R_{p.de}$ indicates near to strong relation between PKA and DSA, ELGAMAL It suggests that PKA algorithm depends on DSA and ELGAMAL.

- **2048 bit length**

$R_{p.rd}$ = 0.73

The result of $R_{p.rd}$ indicates near to strong relation between PKA and RSA, DSA. It suggests that PKA algorithm strongly depends on RSA and DSA.

$R_{p.re}$ = 0.98

The result of $R_{p.re}$ indicates strong relation between PKA and RSA, ELGAMAL. It suggests that PKA algorithm strongly depends on RSA and ELGAMAL.

$R_{p.de}$ = 0.36

The result of $R_{p.de}$ indicates near to weak relation between PKA and DSA, ELGAMAL It suggests that PKA algorithm weakly depends on DSA and ELGAMAL.

Windows 7

1) **Character wise**

- **512 bit length**

$R_{p.rd}$ = 1.00

Multiples Correlation coefficient between three algorithms (PKA is considered as dependent variable and RSA and DSA are considered as independent variable) is Perfect and Possible, because linear correlation exist between all of two variables.

$$R_{p.re} = 1.00$$

Multiples Correlation coefficient between three algorithms (PKA is considered as dependent variable and RSA and ELAGAMAL are considered as independent variable) is Perfect and Possible, because linear correlation exists between all of two variables.

$$R_{p.de} = 1.00$$

Multiples Correlation coefficient between three algorithms (PKA is considered as dependent variable and DSA and ELAGAMAL are considered as independent variable) is Perfect and Possible, because linear correlation exists between all of two variables.

- **1024 bit length**

$$R_{p.rd} = 0.61$$

The result of $R_{p.rd}$ indicates near to strong relation between PKA and RSA, DSA. It suggests that PKA algorithm depends on RSA and DSA.

$$R_{p.re} = 0.61$$

The result of $R_{p.re}$ indicates near to strong relation between PKA and RSA, ELGAMAL. It suggests that PKA algorithm strongly depends on RSA and ELGAMAL.

$$R_{p.de} = 0.43$$

The result of $R_{p.de}$ indicates near to Moderate relation between PKA and DSA, ELGAMAL It suggests that PKA algorithm moderately depends on DSA and ELGAMAL.

- **2048 bit length**

$$R_{p.rd} = 0.59$$

The result of $R_{p.rd}$ indicates moderate relation between PKA and RSA, DSA. It suggests that PKA algorithm strongly depends on RSA and DSA.

$$R_{p.re} = 0.52$$

The result of $R_{p.re}$ indicates moderate relation between PKA and RSA, ELGAMAL. It suggests that PKA algorithm moderately depends on RSA and ELGAMAL.

$$R_{p.de} = 0.58$$

The result of $R_{p.de}$ indicates Moderate relation between PKA and DSA, ELGAMAL It suggests that PKA algorithm moderately depends on DSA and ELGAMAL.

2) Line wise

- **512 bit length**

$$R_{p.rd} = \text{Impossible}$$

Multiples Correlation coefficient between three algorithms (PKA is considered as dependent variable and RSA and DSA are considered as independent variable) is impossible, because linear correlation does not exist between all of two variables.

$R_{p.re}$ = Impossible

Multiples Correlation coefficient between three algorithms (PKA is considered as dependent variable and RSA and ELAGAMAL are considered as independent variable) is impossible, because linear correlation does not exist between all of two variables.

$R_{p.de}$ = 0.61

The result of $R_{p.de}$ indicates Moderate relation between PKA and DSA, ELGAMAL It suggests that PKA algorithm moderately depends on DSA and ELGAMAL.

- **1024 bit length**

$R_{p.rd}$ = 0.56

The result of $R_{p.rd}$ indicates moderate relation between PKA and RSA, DSA. It suggests that PKA algorithm moderately depends on RSA and DSA.

$R_{p.re}$ = 0.92

The result of $R_{p.re}$ indicates strong relation between PKA and RSA, ELGAMAL. It suggests that PKA algorithm strongly depends on RSA and ELGAMAL.

$R_{p.de}$ = 0.93

The result of $R_{p.de}$ indicates strong relation between PKA and DSA, ELGAMAL It suggests that PKA algorithm strongly depends on DSA and ELGAMAL.

- **2048 bit length**

$R_{p.rd}$ = 0.89

The result of $R_{p.rd}$ indicates strong relation between PKA and RSA, DSA. It suggests that PKA algorithm strongly depends on RSA and DSA.

$R_{p.re}$ = 0.27

The result of $R_{p.re}$ indicates weak e relation between PKA and RSA, ELGAMAL. It suggests that PKA algorithm moderately depends on RSA and ELGAMAL.

$R_{p.de}$ = 0.88

The result of $R_{p.de}$ indicates Strong relation between PKA and DSA, ELGAMAL It suggests that PKA algorithm strongly depends on DSA and ELGAMAL.

3) Paragraph wise

- **512 bit length**

$R_{p.rd}$ = 0.61

The result of $R_{p.rd}$ indicates Moderate relation between PKA and RSA, DSA It suggests that PKA algorithm moderately depends on RSA and DSA.

$R_{p.re}$ = 0.61

The result of $R_{p.re}$ indicates Moderate relation between PKA and RSA, ELGAMAL It suggests that PKA algorithm moderately depends on RSA and ELGAMAL.

$R_{p.de}$ = 0.47

The result of $R_{p.de}$ indicates near to Moderate relation between PKA and DSA, ELGAMAL It suggests that PKA algorithm is Moderate depends on DSA and ELGAMAL.

- **1024 bit length**

$R_{p.rd}$ = 0.46

The result of $R_{p.rd}$ indicates moderate relation between PKA and RSA, DSA. It suggests that PKA algorithm moderately depends on RSA and DSA.

$R_{p.re}$ = 0.63

The result of $R_{p.re}$ indicates near to strong relation between PKA and RSA, ELGAMAL. It suggests that PKA algorithm is some Strong depends on RSA and ELGAMAL.

$R_{p.de}$ = 0.46

The result of $R_{p.de}$ indicates moderate relation between PKA and DSA, ELGAMAL It suggests that PKA algorithm moderately depends on DSA and ELGAMAL.

- **2048 bit length**

$R_{p.rd}$ = 0.61

The result of $R_{p.rd}$ indicates moderate relation between PKA and RSA, DSA. It suggests that PKA algorithm moderately depends on RSA and DSA.

$R_{p.re}$ = 0.93

The result of $R_{p.re}$ indicates strong relation between PKA and RSA, ELGAMAL. It suggests that PKA algorithm is strong depends on RSA and ELGAMAL.

$R_{p.de}$ = 0.26

The result of $R_{p.de}$ indicates weak relation between PKA and DSA, ELGAMAL It suggests that PKA algorithm is weak depends on DSA and ELGAMAL.

Windows 8

1) **Character wise**

- **512 bit length**

$R_{p.rd}$ = 0.17

The result of $R_{p.rd}$ indicates weak relation between PKA and RSA, DSA It suggests that PKA algorithm is weak depends on RSA and DSA

$R_{p.re}$ = 0.33

The result of $R_{p.re}$ indicates weak relation between PKA and RSA, ELGAMAL It suggests that PKA algorithm is weak depends on RSA and ELGAMAL

$R_{p.de}$ = 0.61

The result of $R_{p.de}$ indicates Moderate relation between PKA and DSA, ELGAMAL It suggests that PKA algorithm moderately depends on DSA and ELGAMAL

- **1024 bit length**

$R_{p.rd}$ = 0.56

The result of $R_{p.rd}$ indicates moderate relation between PKA and RSA, DSA. It suggests that PKA algorithm moderately depends on RSA and DSA.

$R_{p.re}$ = 0.66

The result of $R_{p.re}$ indicates near to strong relation between PKA and RSA, ELGAMAL. It suggests that PKA algorithm is some Strong depends on RSA and ELGAMAL.

$R_{p.de}$ = 0.33

The result of $R_{p.de}$ indicates near to weak relation between PKA and DSA, ELGAMAL It suggests that PKA algorithm is weak depends on DSA and ELGAMAL.

- **2048 bit length**

$R_{p.rd}$ = 0.51

The result of $R_{p.rd}$ indicates moderate relation between PKA and RSA, DSA. It suggests that PKA algorithm moderately depends on RSA and DSA.

$R_{p.re}$ = 0.50

The result of $R_{p.re}$ indicates moderate relation between PKA and RSA, ELGAMAL. It suggests that PKA algorithm moderately depends on RSA and ELGAMAL.

$R_{p.de}$ = 0.51

The result of $R_{p.de}$ indicates moderate relation between PKA and DSA, ELGAMAL It suggests that PKA algorithm moderately depends on DSA and ELGAMAL.

2) Line wise

- **512 bit length**

$R_{p.rd}$ = 0.61

The result of $R_{p.rd}$ indicates moderate relation between PKA and RSA, DSA It suggests that PKA algorithm moderately depends on RSA and DSA

$R_{p.re}$ = 0.61

The result of $R_{p.re}$ indicates moderate relation between PKA and RSA, ELGAMAL It suggests that PKA algorithm moderately depends on RSA and ELGAMAL

$R_{p.de}$ = 0.47

The result of $R_{p.de}$ indicates near to Moderate relation between PKA and DSA, ELGAMAL It suggests that PKA algorithm moderately depends on DSA and ELGAMAL

- **1024 bit length**

$R_{p.rd}$ = 0.23

The result of $R_{p.rd}$ indicates weak relation between PKA and RSA, DSA. It suggests that PKA algorithm is weak depends on RSA and DSA.

$R_{p.re}$ = 0.24

The result of $R_{p.re}$ indicates weak relation between PKA and RSA, ELGAMAL. It suggests that PKA algorithm is weak depends on RSA and ELGAMAL.

$R_{p.de}$ = 0.17

The result of $R_{p.de}$ indicates weak relation between PKA and DSA, ELGAMAL It suggests that PKA algorithm is weak depends on DSA and ELGAMAL.

- **2048 bit length**

$R_{p.rd}$ = 0.70

The result of $R_{p.rd}$ indicates moderate relation between PKA and RSA, DSA. It suggests that PKA algorithm moderately depends on RSA and DSA.

$R_{p.re}$ = 0.43

The result of $R_{p.re}$ indicates near to moderate relation between PKA and RSA, ELGAMAL. It suggests that PKA algorithm moderately depends on RSA and ELGAMAL.

$R_{p.de}$ = 0.67

The result of $R_{p.de}$ indicates moderate relation between PKA and DSA, ELGAMAL It suggests that PKA algorithm moderately depends on DSA and ELGAMAL.

3) Paragraph wise

- **512 bit length**

$R_{p.rd}$ = 0.41

The result of $R_{p.rd}$ indicates Moderate relation between PKA and RSA, DSA It suggests that PKA algorithm moderately depends on RSA and DSA.

$R_{p.re}$ = 0.41

The result of $R_{p.re}$ indicates Moderate relation between PKA and RSA, ELGAMAL It suggests that PKA algorithm moderately depends on RSA and ELGAMAL.

$R_{p.de}$ = 0.41

The result of $R_{p.de}$ indicates near to Moderate relation between PKA and DSA, ELGAMAL It suggests that PKA algorithm moderately depends on DSA and ELGAMAL.

- **1024 bit length**

$R_{p.rd}$ = 0.37

The result of $R_{p.rd}$ indicates moderate relation between PKA and RSA, DSA. It suggests that PKA algorithm moderately depends on RSA and DSA.

$R_{p.re}$ = 0.65

The result of $R_{p.re}$ indicates near to strong relation between PKA and RSA, ELGAMAL. It suggests that PKA algorithm is some Strong depends on RSA and ELGAMAL.

$R_{p.de}$ = 0.50

The result of $R_{p.de}$ indicates moderate relation between PKA and DSA, ELGAMAL It suggests that PKA algorithm moderately depends on DSA and ELGAMAL.

- **2048 bit length**

$R_{p.rd}$ = 0.48

The result of $R_{p.rd}$ indicates near to moderate relation between PKA and RSA, DSA. It suggests that PKA algorithm moderately depends on RSA and DSA.

$R_{p.re}$ = 0.96

The result of $R_{p.re}$ indicates strong relation between PKA and RSA, ELGAMAL. It suggests that PKA algorithm is strong depends on RSA and ELGAMAL.

$R_{p.de}$ = 0.75

The result of $R_{p.de}$ indicates near to strong relation between PKA and DSA, ELGAMAL It suggests that PKA algorithm is some strong depends on DSA and ELGAMAL.

Chapter -5

Summary and Future Work

5.1 Summary

This study represents the importance of Encryption and decryption of data for storage and transmission. The significance of encrypted data can be identified in light of the mushrooming applications and globalization of communication. The advantages of encrypting data manifest themselves in the form of security & confidentiality in real time applications. Encryption of data is of particular significance in applications like email, e-commerce, e-cash where highly vulnerable communication lines is accessed for transmission of highly volatile data.

The study traces the development and Analysis of various encryption algorithms in a real time environment in all their breath taking diversity and breakthroughs in Chapters 2. The significance of the advances and adaptabilities is measured in terms of their diversity of applications in myriad ways that we feel in our daily lives.

The chapter 3 identifies the methodology used in the developed work. It is classified as algorithm. This algorithm generates a sequence, followed by model to generate sub keys and mapping of sequence or the sub keys on plain text to generate cipher text. . In order to understand the impact of newly developed algorithm on RSA, DSA and ELGAMAL, multiple correlation coefficients are calculated in various operating systems and for different bit length data.

A comparative study of all the developed models is discussed in chapter 4. The developed model is studied in terms of computing power, Avalanche effect and complexity of the models in terms of their construction and strength. A crypto analytical study of all developed model is also considered. PK algorithm is compared with standard block cipher RSA, DSA, and ELGAMAL.

5.2 Conclusions

The conclusions drawn above, reflecting the overall security and confidentiality rates of transmitting data, confirm the improvement in the efficiency of transmitting data. The methodology used in the dissertation can be used for evaluating new encryption algorithms in terms of multiple parameters. Further, the quantitative data indicates relationship between

Random key considered, sub keys generated, computational power needed by this algorithm and the strength and security of the algorithm. It also identifies the importance of multiple parameters like keys, time stamps and nonce values used in algorithm in terms of its security & strength. In the case of Substitution encryption algorithms, the gain by using RSA and ELGAMAL algorithms are their low computational powers, which will be very much gained by using the developed models. The developed models are giving almost equal security at low computational overhead (Computing power). As the security of encrypting models is directly related to the key length, the more the key length the more will be the security of the algorithm. But this parameter increases the computational overhead (computing power) of the encryption algorithms. The security of the developed models is relatively free from the key length which gives more flexibility regarding computing power.

Another conclusion from the above study is freeness from public key attacks. With probabilistic encryption algorithm, a crypto analyst can no longer encrypt random plain texts looking for correct cipher text. Since multiple cipher texts will be developed for one plain text, even if he decrypts the message to plain text, he does not know how far he had guessed the message correctly. Under this scheme, different cipher texts will be formed for one plain text. Also the cipher text will always be larger than plain text.

This process of improvement has been spurred on by the ever-growing user demand for security to the transmission (and storage) of information. The Postwar II period ushered in a new multifaceted era of advances in science and technology;

Emergence of multinational corporations; and globalization of economic activity. This

Change has and will continue to put heavy user demand on security to data in communication systems and networks. Increased competition globally in the e-commerce and other applications underlines the need for secured communication. For data storage and transmission, encryption becomes imperative for security and confidentiality.

5.3 FUTURE WORK:

The present work deals with plain text being represented by numerical and characters of English alphabet. The work can be improved so that it can support the characters of not only English but also of other languages as well.

Considering the future of technology, fields like artificial intelligence and virtual reality will gain major grounds and will become a part of daily life. As a result of that new forms of input like input from gestures, eye movements and even in the form of brain waves can become very common as compared to traditional input means of today.

With these new forms of inputs there arises a new need to secure them for the purpose of transmission and storage. The future work of this algorithm can incorporate the encryption and decryption of these new forms of inputs thereby assuring security of future technologies.

Appendix A
Appendix A. List of Publications by Author

1) Mr.Pratik Vanjara, Dr. Kishor Atkotiya Indian Journal Of Research –
Paripex ISSN- 2250 —1991 August 2012 volume 1, issue- 8
Title: - An Approach to enhance Image Encryption Using Blockbased
Cryptography Algorithm

2) Mr.Pratik Vanjara, Dr. Kishor Atkotiya, Indian Journal Of Research –
Paripex ISSN- 2250 —1991 September 2012 volume 1, issue- 9
Title: - Analysis & Design Graphical Password Authentication Using
Cryptography algorithms

3) Mr.Pratik Vanjara, Dr. Kishor Atkotiya, Indian Journal Of Research –
Paripex ISSN- 2250 —1991 February -2013 volume 2, issue- 2
Title: - An Investigation into the field of cryptography and cryptographic
        algorithm protocols

Bibliography

1) Cryptography: From Black Art to Popular Science, Nader Alosaimi, University Of St. Andrews page [4]
2) development of block cipher modes of operations, Dr.Ali Makki Sagheer, page [1], [2]
3) counter mode development for block cipher operations Ahmed T. Suod, Ali M. Sagheer
College of Science, Al-Anbar University, Iraq,College of Computer, Al-Anbar University, Iraq
Received:18/6/2009 Accepted:28/4/2010
page[1]
4) http://dancalloway.com/wordpress/2009/08/introduction-to-cryptography-and-its-role-in-network-security-principles-and-practice/ ,Introduction to Cryptography and its role in Network Security Principles and Practice, on 08.06.09, in Technology, By Dan Calloway

5) http://en.wikipedia.org/wiki/Ciphertext

6) lecture notes on cryptography shafi goldwasser, mihir bellare page[14]

7) http://www.ukessays.com/essays/computer-science/computer-science-and-electrical-engineering-computer-science-essay.php
8) http://www.garykessler.net/library/crypto.html
9) http://en.wikipedia.org/wiki/Data_Encryption_Standard
10) Lecture 4 data encryption standard (des) slide no 3
11) http://www.rsa.kz/node/glossary/defaultb081.html?id=1045
12) http://www.diablotin.com/librairie/networking/puis/ch06_04.htm
13)http://www.princeton.edu/~achaney/tmve/wiki100k/docs/ElGamal_encryption.html
14) http://www.herongyang.com/Cryptography/DSA-Introduction-What-Is-DSA-Digital-Signature-Algorithm.html
15) Statistical method by S P Gupta
16) http://scialert.net/fulltext/?doi=itj.2013.1818.1824
17) http://computerfun4u.blogspot.in/2009/02/drawbacks-of-using-digital-signature.html
18) Hans Delfs, Helmut Knebl. —Introduction to ryptography:Principles and Applications‖ . Tsinghua University Press, 2007.10.
19)] Ranjan Bose. —Information Theory, Coding and Cryptography‖ ,China Machine press, 2004
20)] Willian Stallings, —Cryptography and Network Security: principlesand Practice‖ . Tsinghua University Press, 2002.6.

21) P. Gutmann, ―Cryptographic Security Architecture: Design and Verification‖ . Springer-Verlag,2004.

22) http://securitycerts.org/review/cryptography-authentication.htm

23) http://www.ascii-code.com/

24) http://sofia.cs.vt.edu/cs1114-ebooklet/chapter4.html

25) Statistical Method : D. C Sancheti & V.K. Kapoor